COLONIALISM
1870-1945

COLONIALISM 1870-1945

An Introduction

D. K. Fieldhouse

Weidenfeld and Nicolson
London

Copyright © 1981 by D.K. Fieldhouse

First published in Great Britain by
George Weidenfeld and Nicolson
91 Clapham High Street
London SW4

ISBN 0 297 77873 0

Printed in Great Britain by
Butler & Tanner Ltd, Frome and London

Contents

Preface   vii

I. Colonialism 1870-1945   1
1. Introduction: Colonialism in its historical
and conceptual context   1
2. Colonialism as political subordination   11
3. The balance sheets of colonialism   41

II. The Economics of Colonialism   51
1. The issues   51
2. The character of an imperial economy   53
3. Agriculture and industry in a colonial
environment   78
4. Conclusions   103

III. The Historiography of Modern Colonialism
1870-1945   109
1. Changing approaches to colonialism   109
2. A short bibliography of modern colonialism   124

IV. A Short Chronology of Colonialism
1870-1945   138

Index   149

Preface

The character of this book was determined by the fact that it was originally commissioned by the Italian publisher Laterza & Figli as one of a series of small volumes, each of which would provide an introduction to a different field of study. Thus, the limits of the subject matter were set by the fact that other volumes in the series – *Libri del Tempo Laterza* – would deal with related topics or periods: in this case there were to be volumes on imperialism and on colonialism after 1945. The common format of the series required a general introductory essay of the type characteristic of a large encyclopedia; a more specialized essay on some major aspect of the subject; a critical bibliography and a short chronology. The book was to be written on the assumption that the reader had little or no initial knowledge of the subject, but wanted a guide to the central issues and to the main literature.

In writing the book I had to bear in mind that comparatively little has been published in Italy on modern colonialism, apart from a substantial literature on the one-time Italian colonies in Africa; and also that Italian readers were likely to be unfamiliar with facts and concepts widely understood in Britain and other countries where the study of modern imperialism and colonialism was more widespread. As a result British readers may find much here that strikes them as elementary, obvious or over simplified. Yet although, as the bibliography makes clear, the literature in English on colonialism is vast, there seems to be no short, simple and accessible book which provides an easy entry into the subject apart, that is, from the many recently published books based on Marxist principles which treat colonialism as the root of 'dependence' and poverty in 'the third world'. This book is therefore published in English, in a slightly revised version, in the hope that, despite its limitations, it may be useful to newcomers to the subject and also suggest that there is a viable alternative to the Marxist view of modern colonialism.

I. Colonialism
1870-1945

1. Introduction: Colonialism in its historical and conceptual context

Colonialism is one of four words widely used to describe different aspects of the control exercised by one society over another. Like all similar terms of art it is neither precise nor self-explanatory and it can only be understood in relation to other closely related terms – imperialism, colonization and neo-colonialism. In fact all these may be seen as describing successive parts of an historical cycle: imperialism results either in colonization or colonialism and each in turn may lead to neo-colonialism. These words, and the realities they attempt to describe, are not, of course, unique to the modern period: one can talk of imperialism, colonization and decolonization leading to neo-colonialism in the ancient or the early-modern world. But this book is concerned only with the period from about 1870 to 1945, so what follows will relate specifically to that period and to the relationships between those states of Europe and North America which possessed colonies in this era and those less-developed countries which, in various forms, came under their control. It is proposed to begin by attempting brief definitions of each of these terms so that modern colonialism can be seen in its true chronological and conceptual perspective.

i. Imperialism

Imperialism is the most widely used of these four concepts and can be regarded as an umbrella word comprehending the whole gamut of relations between a dominant and a subservient society. The difficulty in defining it is that it has meant all things to all men. In a very general sense it can be used to indicate the tendency of one society or state to control another, by whatever means and for whatever purpose. But usually it is given a specific meaning which reflects a particular view of the causes and character of this control.

Three contrasting usages predominate. First, since the publication in 1916 of V.I. Lenin's book, *Imperialism, the Highest Stage of Capitalism*, Marxists have used imperialism to indicate a certain stage in the evolution of modern capitalism, a stage in which the concentration of the ownership of the means of production and exchange had resulted in monopoly capitalism. In Lenin's argument the 'finance capitalists' who then controlled capital found it necessary to divide the world between them, first into commercial empires, then into political empires, in order to safeguard their monopoly of markets and sources of raw materials. Thus colonialism, indicating the condition of dependent societies within these political empires, was both an historical product and also an aspect of 'capitalist imperialism' and would continue until capitalism itself was replaced by socialism. Since, however, these political or 'formal' empires in fact disappeared during the thirty years after 1945, while western capitalism continued, later Marxists have had to modify Lenin's argument, holding that decolonization merely indicated that finance capital had altered its techniques of control. The ex-colonies remained economically subservient, even though nominally independent, and this condition is commonly labelled neo-colonialism.

The essential feature of this definition of imperialism is that it was inevitable: indeed, Lenin was scathing about those socialists who regarded imperialism as an option for modern states.[1] But Marxists are not alone in thinking that domination by richer and stronger states over poorer and weaker societies was historically inevitable. A second usage of the word reflects belief that imperialism was an inevitable consequence of the disproportionate industrial and political power established by Europe and North America in the nineteenth and early twentieth centuries, though not specifically of monopoly capitalism. Thus some historians have denied that any significant number of Europeans ever wanted to govern Africa, Asia or the Pacific: that is, they were not in any sense positive imperialists. But, as European activities in many parts of these regions intensified, so it became apparent that it was impossible for European governments to ignore the political consequences of these proliferating contacts. On the one hand Europeans of different nationalities were coming into conflict on this 'periphery'; on the other few indigenous governments or social structures could for long operate effectively once the pressure of alien interference became intense. Colonialism was the consequence of these two difficulties. The world was divided geographically to resolve conflicts of interest between the powers; formal political rule was imposed to stop chaos and to provide a satisfactory framework for European enterprises of all kinds. Ultimately decolonization came when and because under colonial rule these non-European societies had reached (or were thought capable of reaching) a level of efficiency which would enable them to stand on their own feet as sovereign states.

This 'peripheral' approach to imperialism assumes that most imperialists were 'reluctant'. But there have always been other commentators and historians who argued that imperialism was an act of will and constituted a deliberate choice on the part of the imperialists. Thus imperialism has been defined as 'the deliberate act or advocacy of extending or maintaining a state's direct or indirect political control over any other inhabited territory'. This definition does not, of course, say why imperialists should have wanted to act in this way, but the key word 'deliberate' suggest rational decision. This formulation can, therefore, conveniently be used to represent a wide range of explanations of imperial expansion which emphasize positive and calculated assessment of its rewards, making colonialism strictly functional. A comprehensive list would be very long, but it would certainly include the following: the need of a major power for naval and military bases overseas; concern to protect areas deemed to be of national importance (such as lines of communication) from occupation by some rival power; protection of the frontiers or interests of existing overseas possessions; support for European settlers; the dictates of diplomacy; and aggressive, jingoistic nationalism, possibly what J.A. Schumpeter described as an 'atavistic' urge for unlimited territorial acquisition.[2] What all these have in common is that the European states concerned could equally well have decided not to acquire territory overseas, even though the cost of abstinence might have been high. As a consequence, the end of imperialism and of formal empire would come when the imperialists changed their minds, when they no longer felt these specific impulses or pursued these particular objectives.

The character and roots of imperialism thus remain a matter of controversy; and, because imperialism is the cause of colonialism, so also does the nature of colonialism. To Marxists imperialism, colonialism and neo-colonialism all express the changing character of the hegemony exercised by the capitalist West over the rest of the world. To non-Marxists imperialism and its consequences may indicate a reluctant response to otherwise insoluble global problems or the pursuit of specific objectives of various kinds. It is not, therefore, surprising that the account of colonialism given in this book reflects these incompatible explanations of its genesis and is itself necessarily controversial.

ii. Colonization

The outcome of imperialism, whatever its particular motives, might take one of two distinct forms and is therefore properly given two different names, either colonization or colonialism. Historically the first was colonization, which was in use from the sixteenth century onwards and alone of these four terms has always had a favourable connotation. Deriving from the Greek concept of a colony as the movement and permanent settlement of people from one country to another, this was an accurate description of that great movement of the Portuguese, Spanish, English, Dutch, French and other European peoples that began in the late fifteenth century and resulted in the first overseas empires in America, Africa and Asia. The distinctive feature of this colonization was that the immigrants intended to establish societies as similar as possible to those they had left behind: they were not primarily concerned with the indigenous peoples they found overseas. Most settlements were, therefore, established in regions where the indigenous peoples were relatively few or comparatively weak, because otherwise there would have been great difficulty in finding room for the new settlements or defending them, and in places where the climate was reasonably temperate. Most early settlements were in America, both because it met all or most of these conditions and also because it was of comparatively easy access, though there were small permanent Portuguese settlements in Angola and Mozambique and parts of Asia, Dutch settlers at the Cape of Good Hope and in Indonesia, French settlers in the Indian Ocean and Spanish groups in the Philippines. From the late eighteenth century new settlement colonies were set up by the British in Australia and New Zealand and the number of settlers and the extent of their land in southern Africa greatly expanded. The French attempted to establish a similar European colony in Algeria and the list was later extended by British settlements in Central Africa and Italian colonization in North-east Africa.

The special feature of all this colonization was thus the creation of permanent and distinctively European communities in other parts of the world. These were seldom exclusively European because there was always an indigenous population; and in addition many of these settlements found it convenient to import an additional labour force from non-European countries. Before the mid-nineteenth century the need was met by buying African slaves. Britain abolished slavery in 1833 and most other European states followed her example by about 1870. But the need for labour continued and it was commonly met by importing technically free workers, many from Asia, on contract to work for a specified time. As a result of all these factors, most settlement colonies were ethnically complex and in many of them miscegenation resulted in a substantial dilution of ethnic peculiarities. Nevertheless what distinguished true colonization of this type and age from modern colonialism was that the settlers succeeded in transforming a non-European into a fundamentally European country and that, at least at the start, they did not regard their relations with the 'mother country' as in any sense degrading or undesirable. At the margins of colonization there were failures, though in some cases this failure only became evident in the twentieth century. Algeria, Kenya, Rhodesia (Zimbabwe), Angola, Mozambique and Libya can all be seen as places in which European settlers intended at some time to create a permanent European society but where the limited number of immigrants, or the restricted time available before the onset of decolonization, destroyed the effort, leaving essentially African societies with small residual populations of Europeans. In the early 1980s the future of South Africa remained in the balance.

iii. Colonialism

It is now possible to put colonialism into its proper historical and conceptual context as a parallel to colonization. The contemporary use of the word is recent. In the nineteenth century 'colonialism' was used to indicate the general condition of overseas dependencies or the colonial system as a whole, but without any specifically favourable or unfavourable meaning. In Britain it was most likely to be heard in a different sense as 'a colonialism', meaning a turn of speech or an aspect of life typical of British settler societies which amused sophisticates in the metropolis, just as a 'provincialism' amused Londoners. Precisely because 'colonial' was thus associated in the public mind with places such as Australia, rather than with non-settler dependencies such as India (which was not conventionally described as a colony), when the British empire expanded in the later nineteenth century into tropical Africa, South-east Asia and the Pacific the process and the resulting colonial organization tended to be described indiscriminately as 'imperialism'. As late as 1949 President Truman, when announcing his Part Four Programme, described the relationship between an imperial state and its dependencies as 'imperialism – exploitation for foreign profit'. It was only in the early 1950s that a conventional distinction came to be made between imperialism and colonialism. Imperialism was now restricted to the dynamics of empire-building and, for Marxists, to Lenin's 'the highest stage of capitalism' in the more developed countries. Colonialism then emerged as a general description of the state of subjection – political, economic and intellectual – of a non-European society which was the product of imperialism. For example President Sukarno used the word in precisely this sense at the Bandung Conference in 1955, and this has remained its conventional meaning.

Colonialism, therefore, now means the condition of a subject people and is used exclusively of non-European societies when under the political control of a European state or the USA. The essential fact is that the dominant group are alien and remain so, whereas in a 'colonized' country the dominant group are resident. As a result, so the concept of colonialism implies, there is no necessary identity of interest between rulers and ruled: indeed it is normal to think that they are diametrically opposed. In a typical modern tropical dependency the imperial power retained more or less complete authority, whereas in almost all colonized societies the local Europeans were allowed wide autonomy which, in the case of the British empire, led ultimately to sovereignty within the British Commonwealth. In the tropical colony the agents of imperial authority were a small group of expatriates who were appointed to fill posts there and who therefore regarded the colony as merely a place of work (and often an uncomfortable one which they looked forward to leaving) and eventually retired to live in their European home country. Other Europeans in the territory were likely to be managers of foreign-owned mines, plantations, railways, trading companies, banks etc., or alternatively missionaries, teachers, doctors or small-businessmen. However much such men might become attached to the place in which they worked they would always remain alien. So too would the reward of their labours. Individual Europeans sent their savings home to await their retirement. Foreign-owned businesses transferred part at least of their profits to satisfy their shareholders. Hence, in common usage, colonialism means exploita-tion by the foreign society and its agents who occupied the depen-dency to serve their own interests, not that of the subject people.

A further explicit assumption is that the imperialists normally attempted to destroy the culture of a dependency and to replace it by their own. 'Cultural imperialism' was inseparable from alien rule because conformity with the norms of European society was seen as necessary to the process of subordination, at once assisting control and demonstrating its effectiveness. Thus colonialism tended not only to deprive a society of its freedom and its wealth, but of its very character, leaving its people intellectually and morally dis-oriented – what Frantz Fanon has described in *The Wretched of the Earth*.[3]

This is an emotive definition of colonialism, and it is necessarily so because the concept has been developed and used almost entirely by opponents of colonial rule, just as imperialism was given its modern meaning by those who regarded it as one of the least desir-able products of modern capitalism. Value judgements of this kind cannot effectively be challenged on their own ground: if citizens of the one-time tropical dependencies choose to think of the colonial stage of their past in such a way, there is little the historian or analyst can say that will affect their point of view. It would have been equally futile to suggest to a late sixteenth-century Calvinist that there was much to be said in favour of the medieval Roman Catholic church. In each case, however, there is an alternative and quite different approach. This will be developed later in this chapter, but the basis of the argument is as follows. Those who denounce colonialism commonly do so on the basis of three prior assumptions: first, that there was some better alternative actually available at the time; second, that the undesirable features complained of were deliberately intended by the imperialists; third, that the effects were universally deplorable. Such assumptions are natural in the post-colonial period when past subjection may appear to one-time colonial subjects a totally unwarranted slur on their cultural values and the ability of their own people to run their affairs at least as well as the imperialists could do for them. Whether or not this is true, it is necessarily an ex-post verdict based on the character of a colonial society after varying periods of alien rule and may have little relevance to conditions there when colonialism was first established. The India of the late eighteenth century or Nigeria of the late nineteenth century, when these countries were first occupied by the British, bore very little resemblance to the modern states of the same name; nor did the peoples of the dependent countries necessarily see alien rule at the time in the same way as it came to be seen later. A proper view of colonialism must, therefore, take full account of time and change. The important questions, which will be considered below, are why alien rule took the form it did, how it was operated and what consequences it had for the dependent peoples. That is, colonialism must be seen in its context as one aspect of a particular, largely unplanned and, as it turned out, transient phase in the evolving relationship between more and less developed parts of the world in the century after 1870.

iv. Neo-colonialism

Neo-colonialism, like colonialism, is a term of opprobrium. It came into general use only in the 1950s as a consequence of the withdrawal of political control from an increasing number of European colonies; and its implication is that for a less developed country the nominal end of colonialism does not necessarily result in genuine independence. This assumption was not, of course, new, for it resembled the concept of 'informal empire' used in the nineteenth century and Lenin had talked of 'semi-colonies' (Persia, China,

Turkey) and 'commercial colonies' (Argentina and other ex-colonial countries in Latin America). But, as normally used by Marxists in the mid- and later twentieth century, neo-colonialism had more complex implications which derived from current left-wing attitudes to the causes of economic 'underdevelopment'. Although for the most part these theories were formulated after 1945 they must be taken account of here because they refer back to the character of colonialism.

It has always been assumed by most Marxist writers, including historians, that the primary aim and effect of European capitalism in less developed countries was to 'exploit' their indigenous resources. It was, of course, inherent in capitalism to exploit; but it did this in colonies more effectively than in Europe or North America because the whole power of the colonial state was behind the alien capitalist and there were no counter-balancing forces. The result, as portrayed by modern Marxist theorists such as Paul Sweezy, Samir Amin or André Gunder Frank and by historians such as Jean Suret-Canale, was that colonialism actually made the dependencies poorer than they had been before they were occupied. The peasants were forced to produce unprofitable crops for export to satisfy foreign traders and the needs of the metropolis; natural assets such as minerals were extracted; the means of production and exchange fell exclusively into the hands of foreigners, who used monopoly power to exploit both producers and consumers and who transferred their profits overseas instead of investing them in developing the local economy. The total result was that by the end of the colonial period most colonial countries had become fixed as economic 'satellites' of international capitalism, performing subordinate functions as producers of raw materials and as markets for foreign manufactures, utterly dependent on foreign international capitalism for their economic existence. This condition, so recent writers have argued, did not constitute a mere absence of economic development but a positive pathological condition which is now usually called 'underdevelopment'. As C. Furtado put it in 1964, underdevelopment was a concrete and potentially permanent condition characterized by a 'dualistic economy', a low overall level of efficiency, substantial transfer of profit overseas by foreign owners of capital, very little local investment and almost no attempt to develop the pre-capitalist sectors of the domestic economy.[4]

This condition of underdevelopment, it has been argued, though not restricted to territories that have been formal dependencies in the recent past (indeed, much of the literature relates primarily to Latin America), was the almost universal product of modern colonialism. An attempt will be made in Chapter II of this book to evaluate this belief; but in relation to the concept of neo-colonialism the critical question is why such adverse consequences of colonialism, if they did indeed exist, did not end with decolonization. The answer normally given is that, just as colonialism was established in the first place to serve the interests of foreign monopoly capital, so decolonization took place when and because the capitalists felt confident that the colonial society and economy had been so restructured that their interests could be preserved without continued political control. The ground for this confidence was that while the newly independent governments were in theory free to restructure their economic and social systems, few of them in fact were able or willing to do this. Two factors combined to inhibit change. On the one hand the end of formal empire did not necessarily alter the fact that most large-scale commercial enterprises were owned and run by foreigners, usually foreign-based. On the other hand the new indigenous rulers might consider that their own private interests would be best served by continuing to act as allies – 'compradors' is the term often used – of foreign capital, particularly the great multinational companies which would pay them well (bribes, salaries, directorships, etc.) for their collaboration. This enabled foreign capital, particularly multinational companies, to retain and even to expand their activities; and this in turn blocked the way to 'true independence' for the new states. Conversely the only way to true independence and the end of underdevelopment was for these new states to break off relations with international capitalism, to nationalize foreign-owned assets, to establish socialist economies at home and to rely on the more developed socialist states (who are assumed to have no axe to grind) to provide markets, capital and technical assistance. If they did not do so, colonialism would merely be transmuted into perpetual neo-colonialism.

It is now possible to see colonialism (in the conventional sense of the word) in its historical and conceptual context. Colonialism attempts to describe what proved to be a brief and transient condition that was experienced by most parts of Africa, and much of South and South-east Asia and the Pacific, during the period 1870–1945. Historically it was one of three possible results of European imperialism and expansion overseas, the others being colonization by white settlers and some type of informal control. Under colonialism a dependent society was totally controlled by the imperial power. Its government was in the hands of officials of the imperial state, its social, legal, educational, cultural and even religious life was moulded by alien hands and its economy was structured to meet the needs of European capitalism. Decolonization provided a theoretical opportunity for the new states to destroy existing patterns of dependency but unless they took very resolute action they were liable to remain economic satellites of the former imperial state or, more generally, of international capitalism. Thus colonialism was merely one stage in the evolution of international relationships in the modern world whose central theme was the subordination of all countries to the needs of advanced capitalism. Only the destruction of international capitalism as a result of its internal contradictions can be expected to break through this process of natural evolution.

These are, of course, all theoretical assumptions and assertions and all are open to challenge. The purpose of this book is to analyse the character of colonialism within this broad conceptual framework, to see whether the facts fit the theories. The analysis will be divided into two parts, representing two main facets of the colonial situation. First, in the rest of this chapter, colonialism will be examined as a political phenomenon. Here the central questions are the character of colonial rule, what factors determined the techniques adopted by colonial governments and what effects these systems had on the dependent societies. Chapter II then discusses the economic character of colonialism, with particular reference to the assertion that it was incompatible with true economic development.

2. Colonialism as political subordination

It may seem tautological to say so, but it is important to emphasize that the distinctive and most important single feature of modern colonialism was the fact that the colonial powers took full control over the government of the dependent societies within their empires. This was distinctive because it differentiated true colonies on the one hand from other imperial possessions, such as the self-governing British Dominions, and also from legally independent states over which the advanced countries exercised varying degrees of control from outside. The hallmarks of colonialism were that the dependent country could have no direct contact with foreign states, could not belong to the League of Nations or later the United Nations, could not appeal directly to the International Court at The Hague or maintain an independent currency. But these were mere symbols. The reality was that a colonial people lost whatever collective identity it might previously have possessed and became a mere province of a distant empire, which took responsibility for the whole apparatus of government. Thereafter the indigenous society could only re-emerge, probably in an altered geographical form, as part of the process of decolonization in the mid-twentieth century.

For this reason the key to understanding colonialism as an historical phenomenon lies in analysing the character of colonial government and its impact on any one colonial society; and this will involve examination of the main types of dependency and of contrasting systems of administration. But it is essential at the start to grasp one fundamental point: that the imposition of colonial rule very seldom if ever meant the subordination of one 'nation' or nation state to another. The assumption that this was the essence of colonialism comes easily in the later twentieth century when the ex-colonial territories, now full member states of the international community, conceive of themselves in the same terms as the long-established nation states of the West on which they have modelled themselves. It can thus be suggested that, for example, Britain's occupation of Nigeria was analogous to the German occupation of France in 1940, and so an intolerable affront to the dignity of the Nigerian nation. To the extent that any colonial territory did, at the time of its initial occupation, resemble or even see itself as a nation state – that is, as a distinct, integrated political unit, held together and delimited by its common and coextensive culture, institutions and history – to that extent colonialism might be thought to have denied the principle that all nations have the right to be free and independent. In the full sense of a nation, as the West understood the term in the later nineteenth century, it is doubtful whether any modern colony satisfied these criteria. Yet there were a number of more or less clearly distinguishable states that became colonies. They stand out from the rest by virtue of the fact that they emerged after decolonization with much the same geographical boundaries, and possibly also the political, legal, religious and cultural institutions they possessed beforehand. In some of these a record of more or less continuous resistance to alien rule indicated their sense of outrage at losing their independence. To some degree this was true of the Islamic countries of North Africa – Morocco, Algeria, Tunis and Egypt; of Ethiopia (which was itself an empire competing with the Europeans for control of the Horn of Africa and was only an Italian possession for about five years from 1936 to 1941); of Burma and some other ancient states of South-east Asia. All these countries possessed what Arnold Toynbee has described as 'higher religions' and advanced civilizations and had existed, though normally with very different boundaries, as states with effective central governments long before they were occupied by Europeans. Some, notably Egypt, had only recently broken away, in practice though not in international law, from an existing empire (in that case the Ottoman empire) and were themselves showing strong imperialist tendencies at the time when they were involuntarily incorporated into another imperial system. For such states or proto-states colonialism was at all times regarded as a denial of autonomy and was never fully accepted.

These, however, are the exceptions: the great majority of colonial dependencies do not fit this pattern. None of the states now to be found in tropical Africa and few in the East existed in anything resembling their modern form before European occupation. Ghana, for example, is an adopted name for an area with no natural political or ethnic unity which was put together as a single colony, the Gold Coast, by the British during the later nineteenth century. Zaïre is an artefact of the Berlin African Conference of 1884–5, where the powers found it convenient to delineate an area in the centre of Africa to be administered by Leopold II of the Belgians with the name Congo Free State. Even so many of its boundaries were not established until long afterwards. Even Indonesia, most of which, excluding Western New Guinea (West Irian) and the island of Bali, shares a common Islamic culture, was created by the Dutch from a multitude of small states and islands. Clearly it is meaningless to say that these 'states' lost their freedom. Nor was their 'nationhood' outraged, because this idea was quite unknown outside Europe in the normal sense of the word. Loyalties were more specific and generally local: to the person of a ruler, the traditions of a social group, a piece of land or a religious cult. These loyalties might be very strong, quite as powerful as nationalism in European states, and often generated very determined initial resistance to alien occupation. But equally they might not, especially if at first the Europeans were careful not to threaten established authorities and traditional values; and even where there was resistance at first, in Black Africa this seldom continued in its original form once the indigenous political, religious or military authority had been broken. Thus, although some modern anthropologists and historians claim that there was continuity from this 'primary resistance' to alien control through to later 'independence' and nationalist movements, in Africa this rejection of foreign rule was seldom directly related to pre-colonial political or social units. When the inhabitants of the Gold Coast supported Kwame Nkrumah's campaign for independence in the later 1940s and early 1950s it was not to resurrect a legendary Ghana, which had no connection with the Gold Coast, but on two grounds that were the direct product of colonialism. First, because although they belonged to widely differing African groups, they had been made to feel some common interest by being administered as a single British colony. Second, because they were ready to believe the promise made by the new African political leaders that they would be better off once they had achieved independence.

The general point, then, is that if colonialism was morally wrong, it was not in most cases because the colonial empires swallowed up nations which possessed a sense of separate identity as this was felt by contemporary Europeans. It is more accurate to say that the colonial powers, to serve their own convenience, commonly amalgamated a number of previously distinct ethnic, religious and political units to form administratively convenient colonies and that these were often of such a size that a new race of indigenous political leaders could reasonably hope to mould them into nation states. Sometimes these colonies possessed some intrinsic unity, more commonly they did not; and this lack of natural cohesion was eventually to become the most serious political problem facing the post-colonial successor states. The rulers of these states may blame 'tribalism' on the colonial powers and claim that they divided in order to rule. The truth is that in most parts of the world the basic unit of society and government was small because, as in medieval Europe, the physical problem of constructing and preserving large political units was beyond the capacity of rulers with limited technological resources. These problems were partly solved by the rulers of three of the world's largest empires – the Ottoman Turks, the Mughal emperors of India and successive dynasties in China; though in each case the effort to control distant provinces eventually proved too great for these empires as it had for the Roman empire and later the Holy Roman Empire in the West. These three empires were, in any case, the exception. Although there were many aspiring empires and empire-builders in sub-Saharan Africa during the nineteenth century, such as Futa Toro, Al-Haji Umar, Ashanti, Fulani and Bornu in West Africa, these empires tended to be personal to a particularly able ruler and impermanent because of the technical difficulties of sustaining central control once it had been imposed. In short, the concept of a permanent unitary state with fixed frontiers was largely a European importation into other parts of the world and 'nations' based on such concepts and demarcations are the product of colonialism.

This is not, of course, to imply that colonialism was good or necessary for these societies. It is equally arguable that, where the inhabitants of particular regions lacked common characteristics or historical links, it would have been better for them to remain autonomous until and unless the force of historical development generated 'natural' and therefore potentially enduring bonds, as it had done in Europe and parts of Asia. From this standpoint the creation of colonial states constituted an arbitrary break in the historical process, sometimes splitting regions with some natural connection, elsewhere bringing together societies which had no capacity to co-operate; and in either case doing so at a speed that made it impossible for natural forces to operate satisfactorily. In this respect colonialism bequeathed an impossible heritage to the rulers of the new states.

Thus the proper starting point for a study of colonialism is the nature and significance of the novel and artificial political systems imposed onto geographical regions which, for the most part, had been arbitrarily created to suit the needs of the occupying power and to solve conflicts between competing imperialists. It is proposed to analyse these systems of government under four main headings; first, the juridical basis of colonial rule in different types of dependency; second, the essential contradictions in modern colonialism which influenced the patterns of colonial rule; third, problems and institutions common to all or most of the colonial powers; four, the differing systems of government and contrasting attitudes adopted by various European powers. It will then be possible to reach some general conclusions about the significance of these varying systems for the colonial peoples and their relevance to the character and problems of the successor states after they had achieved independence.

i. The juridical basis of colonialism

In terms of their legitimacy in international law there were three distinct categories of dependency in the period 1870–1945.

a. Colonies

Technically one should use the word 'colony' only for those overseas dependencies which were held in full sovereignty by the metropolitan powers. Sovereignty was acquired in many ways, but essentially it required legal action by the imperial state in conformity with its domestic law, coupled with explicit or implicit recognition by other western powers. The form such legal action took varied with the constitution of each European state: in the case of Great Britain it might consist in a proclamation or order in council by the Crown or an act of parliament; in France a presidential decree; in Belgium or the Netherlands an act of parliament. In each case the essential result was that the colony became a full possession of or even (as in the case of some French, Spanish, Portuguese and Dutch territories) an integral part of the parent state and its inhabitants acquired the nationality of the parent state. This did not necessarily mean that they also possessed all the rights held by citizens of the metropolis: some did, some did not and there were many gradations of status even within individual empires. The important consequence of full colonial status was that international law knew no limitation on the sovereignty of the parent state and the colonial subjects possessed no other nationality.

b. Protectorates and protected states

In strict law these were never the possession of or incorporated with an imperial power, but remained 'foreign' to it and their inhabitants were 'protected persons'. Historically and theoretically protectorates and protected states were places which at some time had, or were deemed to have, voluntarily requested or accepted the 'protection' of another power which promised to defend them against all third parties. Sometimes protection was arranged by treaty with a local ruler or a number of rulers, sometimes it was assumed that protection had been accepted tacitly, even though no formal agreement had been signed. From the standpoint of the imperial states the original purpose of establishing a protectorate rather than a formal colony was to achieve a specific objective without commitment to full control or to perpetual responsibility. Often the main aim was to settle international friction concerning a particular territory or, if done unilaterally, to exclude a rival. Thus the French established a protectorate over Tunis in 1881 by the Treaty of Bardo made with the Bey of Tunis to prevent a feared Italian take-over. Tunis became a protected state in which the established ruler, laws and institutions were preserved, even though over time French influence came to permeate most aspects of government. Other comparable protected states were Morocco, the Sultanates of Malaya and the Kingdom of Tonga in the Pacific, all of which retained something resembling their original geographical shape and institutions. But most protectorates were not coextensive with existing states and were built up from a multiplicity of small units. Often the claim of the imperial power to control these was based on treaties made with individual tribal rulers, but few powers bothered to ensure that they obtained the assent of every ruler in the area they wished to claim. Their assent was assumed. Moreover the role of the imperial power in protectorates of this kind, particularly in Africa, changed fundamentally over time. Even if the original aim had been negative – to exclude some foreign rival – and there was no expectation that the protectorate would be administered by imperial agents, European officials tended to expand their functions and encroach on the powers of the indigenous rulers. By about 1914 it would have been difficult for an uninformed observer to know whether territories such as British and German East Africa, Nyasaland, the Cameroons and most of the hinterland of British West Africa were protectorates (as all these were) or formal colonies.

c. Mandates and Trust Territories

Mandates resembled protectorates in that, while they came under the control of individual European states, they were never imperial possessions and their inhabitants retained a separate nationality. An early example was thé Ionian Islands, which were put under British control in 1815 by agreement between Russia, Austria, Prussia and Britain to prevent international friction and were eventually ceded to Greece in 1864 by treaty between the same powers. The modern mandate system, however, dates from 1919 when the victorious allies agreed, on the insistence of President Wilson, that the colonies taken from the defeated powers, Germany and Turkey, should be distributed between the allies but should not be treated as colonies in order to avoid the accusation that the victors had imperialistic aims. The League of Nations claimed the right to allocate and supervise these territories through its Mandates Commission and they were divided into three categories, A, B and C, according to the extent to which they might be absorbed into the imperial system to which they were allocated. The A mandates – Palestine, Iraq, Jordan and Syria – were treated as protected states and were to be made independent as soon as possible, as all were by 1948. The B mandates – Tanganyika, Togoland, the Cameroons and Ruanda-Urundi – were treated as normal protectorates but could not be incorporated with other colonial possessions and were subject to other limitations. The C mandates, which included South-west Africa and Germany's Pacific Islands, became the possessions in all but name of South Africa, Australia, New Zealand and Japan. The only common feature of all mandates was that they were subject to supervision by the Mandates Commission, to which the administering powers had to send annual reports. The Commission had no power to investigate conditions within the mandates; but when the remaining mandated territories, together with a number of one-time Japanese mandates and other possessions in the Pacific, were transferred to the new Trusteeship Council of the United Nations in 1945, the Council had and used powers of investigation.

The significance of the mandate and trusteeship system has been much debated. In each case the actual institution was only a watered-down version of more fundamental proposals made by liberals in Europe and America for establishing universal control by an international organization over all colonial territories on the assumption that no one country could be trusted to act humanely and constructively in less-developed territories under its exclusive control. Internationalization was expected to stop exploitation. Both in 1919 and 1945 these far-reaching proposals were watered down on the insistence of the colonial powers so that they affected only ex-enemy possessions and gave very limited powers to the supervisory authorities: indeed it was inconceivable that either the League or the United Nations could actually have administered the vast colonial systems of that period. In the event it is doubtful whether the mandate system made much difference to the way in which the administering states acted, though it may, for example, have prevented the integration of Tanganyika into a single British East African federation in which the white settlers of Kenya would have had a large influence; and the British colonial authorities maintained that uncertainty about the future of the mandates inhibited long-term investment and development there. At most the mandate system may have established broad standards for the treatment of dependent peoples. The Trusteeship Council exerted greater influence and became a platform for propagating the idea that all colonial dependencies should be prepared for independence as soon as possible.

ii. The contradictions of colonialism

There are two related contradictions or paradoxes at the centre of modern colonialism which must be defined at this point because they underlie the argument of the rest of this chapter. The first contradiction is between the specific and often limited functions empire was intended or believed to fulfil and the fact of full administration of colonial territories. The second is between the character of colonial governments and those conditions which alone might make alien rule tolerable to the subject peoples. These two problems will be outlined here and their significance further developed later.

A peculiar feature of modern colonialism, one of many which distinguished it from earlier European colonization by settlers, was that complete occupation and detailed administration of often very large tropical territories was by no means always necessary to ensure that the imperialists obtained whatever advantages they had looked for when first annexing them. To demonstrate this fully would require detailed analysis of their motives in each particular case, but the point can be made in general terms by arbitrarily dividing the conventional explanations of modern imperialism into two broad categories – political and economic – and considering how far, in each instance, full occupation and administration were intrinsic to the original purposes of empire.

It has been seen above that there were many 'political' grounds on which new colonies or protectorates were claimed in the period before 1914; but, to recapitulate, four common models can be defined, some positive, others negative. Positively colonies might be needed to provide strategic naval, army or (later) air force bases which would enable their owners to act as a world power. Negatively one might claim a territory in order to ensure that no rival power occupied it and might, as a result, be in a position to threaten one's own 'national interests', such as a vital line of sea communications. Diplomacy provided a third possible reason: colonies, or even claims to colonies, were valuable pawns in the game of international relations. Finally colonies might be taken to satisfy national pride or to express what J.A. Schumpeter described as 'an objectless disposition ... to unlimited frontier expansion'.[5] The relative importance of these impulses in particular cases is not significant for the present argument, though few historians would deny that one or other of these was important in many parts of the world during the 'new imperialism' of the years before 1914. The important point is that it was rare that full administration of any large geographical area was essential to the realization of any of these political aims. Diplomatic or nationalistic purposes were achieved once lines demarcating the area annexed had been agreed with the powers and were drawn on the maps. So also was the strategic aim of denying a territory to rivals. Provision of strategic bases admittedly involved physical control over some territory; yet in most cases this area could be very limited. A coastal naval base such as Aden could largely be insulated from its hinterland. Quite small islands, such as those in the Pacific, served very well as naval bases. Alternatively the system of leasing naval bases on the China coast, adopted by most western powers in the 1890s, showed how one could avoid extensive territorial responsibilities; and in the later twentieth century the American base in Cuba and the British base in Cyprus followed this model. In short, it is quite possible to construct a model of imperialism as a strictly political phenomenon which does not involve direct and detailed regulation of the internal affairs of those territories which were considered to be of political importance to the great powers.

When, however, economic objectives can be shown to have been a prime concern of the imperialists the case is somewhat different. Security for trade did not automatically involve full territorial control for the mere act of annexation or declaring a protectorate automatically ensured free access for one's own nationals and insured against monopoly by some other power. But once Europeans wanted more than freedom to trade with coastal areas, arguments for some degree of internal political control were likely to arise. Trade could often only be expanded by building or improving inland communications and by breaking through the restrictive practices of indigenous vested interests, such as the coastal traders of West Africa. Capital investment, whether in communications, mines or plantations, might be thought to require greater political security than was provided by indigenous political systems. White settlers expected a more secure title to land than non-European law and custom provided. Any or all of these considerations was likely to persuade European governments sooner or later to expand the very limited administrative commitments they envisaged when acquiring tropical possessions in the 1880s, both territorially – that is, inland from coastal trading areas – and in terms of their functions – from loose supervision based on treaties with native rulers to some degree of effective control over them.

Clearly, then, in so far as colonialism had economic purposes, it was likely to result in the effective occupation and administration of large colonial territories. Yet the general relevance of this should

not be exaggerated. By far the greater part of the areas that constituted the modern colonial empires was never intensively developed by foreign capital nor occupied by settlers; and even in
individual territories where foreign enterprises were established they
were often localized, so that their needs could have been met without
extending effective administration over the rest of the dependency.
That is, in most places the primary objectives of the imperial power
could have been satisfied without seriously disturbing indigenous
political and social institutions, leaving native peoples alone. Yet
this was almost never done, and the character of modern colonialism
was largely determined by the fact that practically all colonial
governments inexorably destroyed or overlaid indigenous social
and political forms. The reasons for this apparently irrational process are complex, but the most important motives for undertaking
full, comprehensive colonial administration seem to have been as
follows:

a. The need to raise taxes
Once a colonial or protectorate government was established it
needed funds. No European government (with the exception of that
in Italy under Mussolini) was prepared to pay the cost of colonial
administration for more than a short initial period. The local authorities had thus to raise local taxes. To do this they had to assert
effective authority and to establish at least a skeletal administrative system. If, as was common, the subject peoples resisted taxes,
they had to be 'pacified'. In this way the need for revenue drove
all colonial governments to expand their role from supervision to
effective rule.

b. Security
Some indigenous rulers from the start collaborated willingly with
the imperialists, often because they expected some advantage from
alliance with an obviously powerful new force. But others did not;
and the need to safeguard the frontiers of the area effectively
occupied was a ground for suppressing dissidents and imposing full
control.

c. The ambitions of soldiers and administrators
It was an almost invariable rule that those Europeans sent to take control of new colonies felt that their own reputations and careers would be enhanced by success in expanding the effective authority of their parent state. Soldiers, in particular, could hope for promotion only if they could demonstrate their ability and bravery. Their activities were often unauthorized or even forbidden by the authorities in Europe: but their achievements were irreversible. To a large extent the character of the modern colonial empires was formed by 'the men on the spot', for personal motives.

d. 'The civilizing mission'
Among the reasons often given by such men was the moral obligation of Christians from a more advanced civilization to improve 'backward' peoples. This was often genuinely felt and it was one objective which could be expected to receive substantial support in Europe. If it could be shown that the only way in which slavery, infanticide, cannibalism, endemic tribal warfare, and so on could be suppressed and Christianity, education, medical welfare, etc. established was by overcoming local resistance and creating a 'modern' society, it was very difficult for imperial governments to forbid such action. In these and other ways the initial imposition of very limited imperial authority in the new dependencies everywhere evolved into full colonial government and gave colonialism its special character.

Thus the first contradiction within modern colonialism was between the character of empire as it was conceived by most imperialists at the time when colonies or protectorates were first acquired and the character it evolved over the years. To recapitulate, colonialism was initially conceived as involving a strictly limited liability for the imperial power; yet over time that liability became unlimited. From the standpoint of the mass of the people in each imperial metropolis, who had no direct interest in the colonies, this might well alter the whole case for possessing an empire. Mature colonialism was found to involve considerable and apparently endless financial costs to the metropolis: the grants in aid of colonies unable to balance their budget; public investment leading, by the

1940s, to the concept of 'aid' for development; maintenance of inflated armed forces to defend and control the colonies; and ultimately the emotional strain of suppressing nationalist movements with whose objectives many in the imperial states might agree. Here, it can be argued, lay one of the roots of ultimate decolonization: colonialism became discredited among the colonialists themselves because full political control was found to involve unacceptable costs.

The second contradiction or paradox, which is equally relevant to understanding the nature of decolonization, turns on the effects of colonialism on the attitudes of the colonial subjects to alien rule. It has been argued that, because many if not most countries that became colonial dependencies were not, and did not see themselves as, nation states, alien rule might often be accepted as another variant of the overrule or paramountcy common in non-European societies. But the condition for such acceptance was that, on the one hand, the imperialists should not radically interfere with the values and institutions indigenous to these societies; and, on the other, that their fundamental attitudes should not be so reconstructed that they came to see their predicament as Europeans in the same situation might have done. Colonialism in fact broke both conditions for its success. On the one hand it caused resentment by what it destroyed; on the other hand it encouraged its subjects to think as Europeans, and in so doing narrowed the gap between rulers and ruled. Once a sufficient minority of them had acquired European skills and adopted European assumptions about, for example, freedom and equality, alien rule would seem as intolerable an anomaly as that of one European state by another. By the mid-twentieth century, and long before then in dependencies such as India, Ceylon (Sri Lanka) and Indonesia which had had the longest exposure to colonialism, this process had reached the point at which alien rule became fundamentally unstable; and by that time also most imperial countries were beginning to find the burden of empire as they had constructed it intolerable. In these ways and for these reasons modern colonialism contained the seeds of its own destruction and decolonization was the inevitable outcome. Some of these problems are discussed in the following section.

iii. Common problems and institutions

a. The problem of government

Although at the start of the modern colonial period few men perceived these underlying contradictions, all colonial administrators quickly became aware that it was extremely difficult to find any really satisfactory method of controlling the new tropical dependencies. The main problem was not, in fact, physical resistance to alien rule. This was widespread at the start and was never entirely eliminated. But it could everywhere be suppressed or contained because the imperialists possessed far superior military resources and better political organization and there were no external powers to support resistance movements, as there were to be after 1945. The real and never resolved problem was how the occupying power could sustain effective control once it had been established. On the one extreme, reliance on overwhelming military or para-military power was out of the question. It would have been far too expensive and, at least in the West European democracies, governments were vulnerable to criticism of brutality by liberals and humanitarians, such as the British Anti-Slavery Society. Force had to be available and was used where necessary, but it could not be the basis of day-to-day rule: for that acquiescence and some degree of collaboration were essential. At the other extreme, however, the traditional system of all British settler colonies (and to a lesser extent of other European possessions in America) whereby the settlers largely ran their own affairs using the institutions and laws of the metropolis, was clearly impracticable in the tropical dependencies, at least for a long time after they were first annexed. None possessed any tradition of parliamentary government and few conceived of public administration as the West understood it. Anything resembling democracy was therefore out of the question until and unless a colony had undergone basic restructuring. There was the further consideration that the occupying powers could not assume obedience or loyalty and were therefore reluctant to dilute their power. Thus all colonial regimes had to preserve effective control without overt dependence on force and to obtain cooperation without using European constitutional forms. The result was a variety of experimental systems, each adapted to the circumstances of a particular society and influenced by the peculiar approach of individual imperial countries. All depended on co-operation by the colonial peoples, though this was obtained in many different ways that are the hallmarks of the various imperial systems. But all necessarily had two features in common: the backbone of government was the bureaucracy, and both in the metropolis and in the colonies politics played a minimal role in colonial affairs.

It is, indeed, one of the most striking facts about modern colonialism that it aroused so little interest among the public, and therefore also the politicians, of the imperial powers. In a generalized sense, perhaps, there might be pride in empire and passions could sometimes be aroused by international friction over colonial territories. Yet this was less because they were considered important than because the national honour could be made to seem at stake. For the rest, few citizens could have named any significant number of their country's possessions or their characteristics. Such apathy among electors naturally deterred politicians from emphasizing colonial issues, and these normally cut across party groupings. Specific issues might be taken up in parliament for ideological or opportunistic reasons but they never formed the basis of any party's electoral platform and as a rule colonial business emptied parliaments. The French were the only democratic state to allow representatives of their colonies to sit as members of the national assembly and these were too few in number to influence policy.

b. Bureaucracy in the European capitals
The universal result was that the actual control of colonial affairs lay with the bureaucratic departments – the British Colonial Office and the India Office, the French Colonial Ministry, and colonial ministries in the Netherlands, Belgium, Portugal, Germany, Spain and Italy, though these had varying titles reflecting particular concepts of the relationship between colonies and metropolis. Thus in 1937 the Italian Minister of Colonies was given the new title Minister of Italian Africa to reflect the conquest of Ethiopia and for two years, from November 1937 to October 1939, Mussolini himself held this post to emphasize its importance. Apart from one or more political heads, these ministries were staffed by professional civil servants who spent a lifetime on the job and acquired a vast body of knowledge along with many prejudices. They, rather than the political ministers,

whose tenure of office was usually short, moulded the character of modern colonialism. Much recent work has been done on their attitudes and if one feature common to all countries emerges it is that these bureaucrats became deeply concerned for the welfare of the dependencies as they conceived it. Contrary to the assumptions made by most Marxists, officials instinctively and almost invariably put the needs of the subject peoples first, even if this meant rejecting demands and proposals made by economic or other pressure groups in the metropolis or colonies and fighting other departments for a larger share of public funds. In these and many other ways they represented the best features of modern European civil services. Their defects were also typical of bureaucratic departments. They tended to become bound by their own routines and internal structures. They were too anxious to prevent political controversy, more concerned with getting through immediate business than planning for the future. In the British Colonial Office, for example, the underlying assumption concerning the nature and purpose of colonial rule appears to have become ossified around the concept of 'trusteeship' by the time of the First World War. Trusteeship implied that empire entailed a moral responsibility for the welfare and evolution of the 'backward peoples' of the dependencies so that policy must be formulated with their interests in the forefront. While this was a progressive concept around 1900, when many imperialists in all countries assumed that empire should serve the interests of the metropolis first and last, it had become archaic by the later 1930s when the first generation of colonial politicians were beginning to reject the paternalism implicit in trusteeship. Yet it was not until the eve of the Second World War that British officials began seriously to consider how best to stimulate real self-government in tropical dependencies and even after 1945 most still assumed that it would be generations before the colonial peoples could be considered ready for independence.

A parallel limitation in the attitudes of imperial officialdom was that they had a very restricted concept of economic management in the colonies. Themselves probably trained in one of the traditional academic disciplines and suspicious both of contemporary economists and 'big business', they normally assumed that the economic development of the tropical colonies would follow a 'natural' course, except in so far as it was affected by basic metropolitan economic policies such as free trade or protectionism. Occasionally an exceptionally committed or energetic minister, such as Albert Sarraut, who was French Colonial Minister throughout the 1920s, might draw up ambitious plans for investment in and development of the colonial economies for the mutual benefit of colonies and metropolis, as he saw it.[6] Leo Amery as Colonial Secretary in Britain in the later 1920s had comparable ambitions. Their projects foundered on cost and inertia and the slump of the early 1930s discredited plans to expand commodity production in the colonies for an already overstocked international market. Thus it was not until the early 1940s that any colonial ministry began seriously to think of economic development in terms of contemporary growth economics and with the primary aim of correcting defects in colonial economic structures, such as over-dependence on commodity production and inadequate industrialization. Effective action of this type then became characteristic of the last two decades of the colonial period after 1945 and reflected a substantive change in the attitudes of imperial bureaucrats and even some politicians.

c. Bureaucracy in the colonies
Non-political, bureaucratic imperial government at the centres of empire was duplicated in the local colonial administration. Some special features of the British and French systems will be described below, but virtually all government in the tropical colonies had common elements. Since, as has been seen, representative parliaments were very rare before 1945 – India, Ceylon, Indonesia and some West Indian islands were the only dependencies to have these, and even so with many restrictions on their powers – government consisted of officials, appointed and removable by the metropolitan authorities and thus in no sense responsible to those they ruled. In most colonies there was a central council to advise the governor. This might contain a few indigenous representatives, probably nominated rather than elected; but the majority of members were European officials with very limited ability to control the governor or deviate from metropolitan policy. Thus while these councils might constitute a nucleus and growing point for eventual constitutional government, they could not act as an effective focus for colonial politics until they

had been radically transformed, as most were in the decade after 1945. Meantime colonial officials were able to pursue their objectives with minimum concern for the political consequences and the few indigenous politicians found it extremely difficult to obtain a platform. Below the central governments stretched a descending hierarchy of European colonial officials down to the district officer, all career bureaucrats and in many respects resembling the *intendant* of pre-revolutionary France or a Napoleonic *préfet*. Although, as will be seen, these men might be very independent of the central colonial government, real 'kings of the bush', they too thought of government in terms of administration, not politics. For better or worse colonialism in most territories meant absolute rule by Platonic guardians or perhaps enlightened despots of the eighteenth century.

iv. Contrasting attitudes to colonial administration: Britain, France and other powers

In retrospect the common characteristics of all the modern colonial systems that have been outlined above seem more important than differences between the attitudes and practices of individual states. Yet at the time, and still in the mythology of particular European and ex-colonial states, emphasis was placed on differences of approach which expressed the peculiar character of individual countries and colonies. Since there were, in fact, quite important differences which affected the process of decolonization and the position of the successor states, it is proposed briefly to examine some of the distinctive ideas and practices of the two largest modern imperial systems, those of Britain and France. Space makes it impossible to give useful comment on the many other national systems. Material on these is noted in the historiographical essay in Chapter III and a summary account of many of them can be found in my book, *The Colonial Empires.*[7]

a. The British colonial system

Apart from the fact that it was the largest colonial empire and contained the greatest diversity of practice, the British colonial system was distinguished by the interaction of two contradictory traditions. First, there was the tradition of self-government which had been evolved in the colonies of white settlement (Canada, Australia, New Zealand, etc.). Fundamental to this tradition was the belief that each colony was a separate unit which ran its own affairs with minimal supervision from the centre; that English law and institutions should apply unless there were special reasons for withholding them; and that government should be based on representative democracy. Second, there was the tradition of autocratic government which had developed in British India and in a number of colonies in the tropics since the 1790s which were generally known as Crown Colonies. In such places neither British laws nor representative forms of self-government had been thought suitable because the inhabitants were for the most part neither British nor European. Although practice varied widely, common factors were autocratic government by colonial governors, closely supervised by London, and the preservation of existing patterns of law and social organization. The political history of modern British colonialism after 1870 would be determined by the interplay of these two apparently inconsistent traditions.

Fundamentally British policy in the new colonies acquired in Africa, South-east Asia and the Pacific in and after the 1870s was to treat them as Crown Colonies, on the ground that they had few British settlers and were therefore neither entitled to or fitted for self-government. Special methods of controlling them were therefore evolved which will be considered below. Yet it is important to recognize that the alternative tradition of the self-governing settlement colonies had a considerable and, indeed, increasingly important influence on this new dependent empire, emphasizing the difference between British and continental colonialism. Two aspects of this influence were of particular importance. First, the concept of the individuality of each colony: unlike the French, the Americans and the Portuguese, among others, the British never treated the colonies as mere provinces of the metropolis. Each had its own legal personality, constitution, laws and government. Governors were allowed considerable independence from London and local budgets were entirely autonomous. Britain was even reluctant to group colonies into federations: before 1945 the only significant proposal of this kind was for closer union between Uganda, Kenya and Tanganyika in the 1920s, and this foundered on concern that the white settlers of Kenya might gain control. Thus the British empire remained a collection of distinct political units, linked only by common nationality (excluding the protectorates) and by common relations with the metropolis.

The other important idea transferred from the older settlement colonies to these newer Crown Colonies was that government should be influenced by the governed and that the ultimate objective should be representative self-government. In the short term democracy was absolutely excluded. Even so Crown Colonies had legislative councils whose assent was necessary to the passage of local legislation in the form of ordinances. Until 1944 no Crown Colony except Ceylon had a majority of elected representative members on its legislative council, yet all had some non-official members and there was a clearly demarcated track by which a council might eventually evolve into a proper parliament. Thus indigenous politicians could and did claim that representative government was a fundamental principle of the British empire and press for the progressive transformation of the autocratic Crown Colony system of the present into full representative democracy as they saw it in the colonies of British settlement. By the 1940s the tension between these two traditions was becoming acute everywhere and during the following two decades the victory of the self-governing principle was to lead rapidly to decolonization.

But for most of the era of modern colonialism self-government remained a remote, largely theoretical concept. The immediate aim of the British authorities was simply to ensure control of their subject peoples by the best available means; and in the new non-settlement colonies they, in common with other imperial powers, had two very broad alternative techniques to choose between. On the one hand they could rule 'directly', that is, by abolishing or ignoring traditional rulers and institutions and constructing a bureaucracy of paid officials, European at the top, non-European at the lower levels, which ran the colony in much the same way as countries in Europe had been run by officials under the *ancien régime*. The alternative policy was to preserve indigenous political and social structures, to form an alliance with the traditional rulers, and to rule 'indirectly' through them. This second technique had many potential benefits, which will be considered below; and it came eventually to be regarded as the most characteristic of all British approaches to colonial rule. Yet this had not been the invariable or even dominant British policy before 1870 and even during the next seventy years practical problems prevented 'indirect rule' being applied universally. Hence the British empire provides a complete spectrum of systems of government, ranging at one extreme from full 'direct' rule, in which traditional rulers and institutions were abolished or ignored and government was in the hands of officials from top to bottom, to 'indirect' rule at the other extreme in which the British acted as supervisors of traditional authorities.

The classic example of direct rule was in British India (that is those parts of the sub-continent where the Indian princes had been deposed). British India was ruled by a small number (898 in 1893) of members of the Indian Civil Service, most of them British but increasingly Indian after 1920, who exercised their power through a descending hierarchy of minor European and Indian salaried officials down to village level. English was the language of government and therefore of higher education and in many ways the educated Indian elite became anglicized. Direct rule had been adopted gradually during the early nineteenth century when and because it proved impracticable to work through traditional Mughal agents and institutions. Yet there were limits to anglicization. In most respects Indian culture, language and religion survived and local customary law in civil matters was preserved and codified. Moreover India also demonstrated the other end of the spectrum of methods of colonial rule for the many princely states continued to be ruled along largely traditional lines by the established ruling families. Thus, although India provides the classic example of a colonialism that established a fundamentally new system of government and adopted bureaucracy as the best means of obtaining collaboration by Indians in the business of government, it also demonstrates the essential dualism of any colonial system: it must preserve even while it innovates.

All other British dependencies can be placed somewhere along a line that runs from British India to the Indian princely states according to whether a particular country was administered by salaried professional bureaucrats and the colonial subject was treated as an individual; or whether the British acted through indigenous notables and established institutions and individuals were treated as part of a traditional group. It would be a pointless and largely semantic exercise to place all the many British possessions along this line. Broadly, in addition to British India, direct rule was used in varying forms wherever indigenous authorities and social systems had already been weakened or replaced before the concept of indirect rule became widely influential early in the twentieth century, and also where it seemed inconvenient to preserve traditional rulers and systems. On the whole this meant that the colonies acquired earliest were likely to be run in this way: Ceylon, Burma, southern Africa and coastal possessions in West Africa, such as the colonies of Lagos, Sierra Leone and Gambia; together with the very different colonies of Mauritius and the British West Indies. For different reasons relatively late colonies, such as Northern Rhodesia (Zambia), Kenya and Nyasaland (Malawi), retained little of their native political institutions and were ruled bureaucratically. At the other extreme indirect rule in various forms was practised in Nigeria, in the hinterlands of other British West African colonies, in parts of Uganda, Tanganyika, the Malay sultanates, Borneo, Fiji and Tonga, and, in a very different context, in Egypt and Iraq.

Much more important than a precise classification of the system used in particular colonies is the fact that from the early twentieth century the concept of preserving indigenous society, culture and forms of authority became the generally stated and deeply held aim of British colonial policy almost everywhere and this had a far wider impact on colonialism than could be measured in institutional terms. Put negatively, the concept emphasized that non-European peoples had a claim not to be compelled to change their identity; positively, that indigenous social, cultural and political institutions had intrinsic value and should form the basis from which each society could evolve. In the 1920s such views received much support from leading anthropologists such as Bronislaw Malinowski; and to many British imperialists, led by Lord Lugard, who had evolved a system of indirect rule in Nigeria and was its main publicist after his retirement, it seemed that this provided the best solution to the two fundamental problems of colonialism: how to exert a largely unwanted political control over the colonies and how to make alien rule morally defensible.[8] Indirect rule was cheap because it did not need many paid officials and effective because there was little challenge to conservative prejudice. Moreover it could also be progressive because the rulers could be persuaded gradually to abolish practices Europeans found abhorrent (slavery, etc.) and to adopt improved systems of government, taxation, production, etc. Thus the British tended to idealize indirect rule as the solution to most if not all of the practical and ethical problems of colonialism. On this basis empire might last for an indefinite period because it was essentially stable.

Indirect rule, however, had limitations, though many of these only became evident after the event. In particular it made no provision for those indigenous people who acquired education, emancipated themselves from traditional forms of deference and expected to obtain work and respect related to their achievements, not their social origins. Such men found themselves frustrated in most colonies because Europeans monopolized top posts; but it was worst for them in places where archaic social and political systems were bolstered against change by the colonial authorities. Men of this kind received little sympathy from most white officials, who seem to have felt empathy with African chiefs and Indian princes rather than with those educated Africans or Indians who more closely resembled themselves. This may have been partly due to the tendency for officials of middle- or lower-middle-class origin to respect men who bore some resemblance to those European landed gentry on whom they often seem to have modelled themselves, or to fear that 'educated Africans' would challenge their position, as educated Indians had already by the 1920s challenged that of the Indian Civil Service. Whatever the reason, it was not until after 1945 that emancipated Africans were able to break through such obstacles to lead the revolt against conservatism and colonialism and then become leaders of the new states.

Until then their position symbolized the contradiction inherent in all colonialism, but particularly in that of Britain. The British were right to believe that the easiest way to run their colonial empire was to act as the allies of established conservative elites wherever these could be found. With such people the imperialists could make a mutually rewarding deal. Empire preserved the status quo from both internal and external threats; indeed, many indigenous rulers extended their territories and increased their wealth by collaborating with British power: for example, the Kabaka of Buganda in Uganda and the emirs of Northern Nigeria. If they could have insulated such societies from western influence the imperialists might have been able to sustain their rule on this basis for an indefinite period. But they could not, and in fact did not attempt to do so, for the tradition of educating non-Europeans and implanting western and liberal values was as old as European overseas expansion. Just as the *ancien régime* in France was sapped by the tide of liberal thought flowing around the country despite attempts at internal censorship, so colonialism, and in particular indirect rule, was undermined by intellectual contact with the outside world. Well before 1945 it was clear that the educated minority in almost all British possessions would claim the reward of having assimilated themselves to the culture of the imperial power – the right to be treated as Europeans. They could not rightly be denied. The tragedy was that when, after about 1950, the British conceded the legitimacy of this claim and began to prepare the ground for independence, it became clear that by preserving indigenous society in this way nothing had been done to lay foundations for a western-style democratic society. As late as the early 1940s, for example, the Colonial Office had planned to build a multi-tier system of representation with the existing 'native authorities', the partly autonomous indigenous units, as the basis which was explicitly intended to prevent urban politicians from manipulating a conventional electoral system covering the whole colony. By the 1950s this looked merely obscurantist. From that point every sustained tribal loyalty became an obstacle to creating new 'national' loyalties; and the fragmentation of power meant that at the time of independence there were very few who understood the concept of a unitary state. This symbolized the essential dilemma of empire in the tropics. Under colonialism the concept of indirect rule was probably the best device for resolving the basic contradictions of the colonial situation – the often unwelcome need to govern and the need for collaboration by the governed. But indirect rule and conservationism were overtaken by events, many of them outside the colonies. In the end decolonization in British Africa and the Pacific, though not in South or South-east Asia, came perhaps a generation before the new courses adopted after 1945 could reach their goals.

b. *French colonialism*

The ironic element in French colonialism is that, although the French took a different view from the British of the character of their colonies, and in particular of the relationship with metropolitan France, in the end the facts of life in the colonies forced them to follow very similar policies to those found in a number of British territories. That is, the French conventionally believed in direct bureaucratic rule and assimilation to French culture; but they had to make so many concessions to reality that their practices overlapped with the assimilationist end of the spectrum of British colonialism.

The root of France's attitude to her overseas empire was the belief that, as a republic based on the principles of universal liberty, equality and fraternity, it was morally wrong to treat colonies as subordinate possessions of the metropolis. The logic of this position was that overseas territories were integral parts of the French Republic and that all their inhabitants were French citizens possessing the same rights as citizens in France. This in fact was the position adopted by the revolutionary government in Paris in the 1790s. It was modified during the many successive regimes from then until the Third Republic was established in 1871 and some of the more dogmatic elements in the approach had been dropped. Yet the basic assumption of the unity of the Republic and the equality of all its people remained as an ideal; and to the end of the colonial period many Frenchmen regarded any deviation as an undesirable, even if unavoidable, compromise.

In the modern period there were three types of French dependency whose juridical status resembled those of Britain's possessions: *coloniesincorporées*; protectorates or protected states; and, after 1919, mandates. Only the first category were part of the Republic, and even in these colonies citizenship and other rights were complicated and not consistent. All who lived in French colonies were French nationals, but not all were French citizens. Citizenship was supposed to be held by all nationals who qualified by certain tests, including rejection of non-Christian legal and religious principles. Most citizens qualified individually, and few nationals ever did so; but by 1880 all the inhabitants of the Caribbean colonies, Réunion and Tahiti were automatically full citizens by French law. Similar contrasts and inconsistencies existed in forms of government. All full colonies sent deputies to the French Assembly, but only citizens were entitled to vote and in 1936 there were only twenty colonial delegates in a Chamber of 612 – too few to influence policy but enough to enable the French to claim that the colonies assented to legislation through their representatives. For local government the full colonies had elective *conseils généraux* or *conseils coloniaux*, which were modelled on the *conseils généraux* of the departments in the metropolis. They were regarded as a great privilege, yet they were established only in the Caribbean, Réunion, the Pacific and those areas of Algeria and Senegal which had a large concentration of citizens; and even there they had very much less power to legislate or control finance than the British legislative councils. The rest of the French empire had non-representative *conseils d'administration* consisting of senior permanent officials. Federations also had *conseils de gouvernement*, but neither had much power. The nearest thing these territories had to a part-representative legislative council was the *délégations* in Algeria, Madagascar and Oceania (the Pacific islands) and the *grand conseil* of Indo-China, which included some non-Europeans and could produce resolutions on topics such as taxation and public works.

There is thus a paradox at the centre of French colonialism. A republic which believed in equality and representative government allowed the inhabitants of its colonies much less political freedom than the British allowed their colonial subjects. Indeed the whole concept of 'self-government' (the French had to use the British term because there was no French equivalent) was quite alien to French imperial thinking. Principle was served by colonial delegates in the Assembly: the reality was that the colonies were run by professional administrators even more completely than British Crown Colonies that had non-elective legislative councils. In fact this paradox did not worry French imperial theorists because they argued that the present state of affairs was only a transitional stage on the way to full assimilation of the colonies with France. In course of time, as indigenous peoples responded to French influence and became, in effect, Frenchmen, they too would receive these rights and institutions; and since ultimately the Republic would be united by its central parliament, there was no need to emphasize the role of government in each colony.

Assimilation, however, was much more than a process of political unification. Its main content was cultural, combining the eighteenth-century concept of the universality of man with the nineteenth-century belief in both the civilizing mission of Europe and the special value of French culture. In so far as one can measure such things, the French seem to have believed more passionately in this than in any other purpose of colonialism. Yet assimilation had a very limited practical effect on France's overseas possessions and did not even remain the stated object of French policy throughout. Indeed it was so obviously impracticable to transform the millions of Africans and others who came under French rule after the 1870s into coloured replicas of Parisians that colonial administrators evolved a quite different theoretical approach to the aims and methods of colonialism. In the two decades after 1890 men such as Pavie, de Lannesan, Galliéni, Lyautey, Cambon and Harmand worked out or elaborated what they called the principle of *Association*. Harmand, in what became a major text for colonial administrators published in 1910, defined its aims as 'letting [the aborigine] evolve in his own way: maintaining each in his place, his functions, his role; by touching native customs and traditions with a very light hand only and ... using this organization to reach these objectives.'[9] This became the new orthodoxy until the Second World War and was taught systematically to fledgling colonial administrators in the Ecole Coloniale in Paris. By the 1920s professors in the Ecole were preaching the virtues of 'Indirect Rule' as practised in the British colonies and rationalized by Lord Lugard in his book, *The Dual Mandate*, published in 1922. It seemed that French and British colonialism were on converging courses.

This was, in fact, partly an hallucination. French colonial administrators had accepted that the facts of tropical empire made a pragmatic approach essential, but they could neither undo the past nor totally offset the instinctive French approach to colonial administration. By the 1920s the successive generations of French military and civilian rulers had destroyed too much of the indigenous political systems they inherited to adopt indirect rule in its British form. Moreover the hierarchical tradition of French bureaucracy proved indestructible. Although a few of the surviving indigenous kings, chiefs and notables of French possessions were preserved and the pressure to destroy native customs reduced, French colonial rule down to the later 1940s remained essentially bureaucratic, centralizing and assimilationist.

This was the characteristic French approach to the problem of running non-settler dependencies: it was also that of the Portuguese and Americans. It had many virtues from the standpoint of the successor post-colonial states: a centralized and uniform bureaucracy was a more convenient inheritance than a decentralized and variegated structure such as the British left in most of their possessions. Yet the French came no closer than the British to resolving the basic contradictions inherent in colonialism. On the one hand the burden of administering and pacifying such vast areas was disproportionate to any benefits received by France; so that after 1945 few Frenchmen seem to have regretted decolonization except for the army, which had a vested interest, settlers in Algeria and Tunisia, who stood to lose everything, and those nationalists who regarded empire as a necessary symbol of French greatness. On the other hand even the most fully assimilated colonial citizens, more at home in Paris than in Dakar or Saigon, eventually demanded independence. The final result was not an extended multiracial Republic of people speaking French but the end of colonialism.

c. Other colonial systems

The British and French, of course, were only two of many countries that possessed colonies during the modern period. Others include the Dutch, Spanish and Portuguese, all of whom had been colonial powers since the fifteenth and sixteenth centuries; and the Americans, Belgians, Germans and Italians, who had acquired colonies for the first time after 1870 and held them for varying periods: the Germans only until the First World War, the Italians until 1943. Each of these countries had its special approach to colonialism and their ideas and techniques repay detailed study. Space makes it impossible to describe any of them in detail here; and in any case this is unnecessary for a general analysis of the nature of colonialism since in different ways and in varying combinations the various features found in the British and French systems formed the basis of all others.

The basic distinction was again between colonies founded and

developed as part of the process of settler colonization and dependencies based on external power. All these states attempted at one
time or another, in some at least of their overseas possessions, to
stimulate genuine settlement colonies but very few succeeded. There
were substantial blocs of Europeans living permanently in American
Hawaii and Puerto Rico, in Dutch Java, in Portuguese Mozambique
and Angola (which from the 1920s were treated as an integral part
of the mother country), in German South-west and East Africa and
in Italian Libya and other parts of North-east Africa. At various
times these imperial states evolved policies aimed at large-scale
emigration and settlement, often at great cost (notably the Italian
settlement schemes under Mussolini, possibly the most expensive in
relation to the number of colonists and the area settled in the whole
of colonial history). Several states also conceived schemes for in-
tegrating these and other overseas possessions with the metropolis,
much as France did. In the event colonization almost always failed
to create predominantly European societies and few of these integra-
tionist projects came to anything. Hawaii became a state of the
Union in 1959 and Puerto Rico remained a commonwealth closely
associated with the USA. The small Portuguese and Spanish islands
in the Atlantic were integrated with these states, as were the French
Caribbean territories and Réunion with France and the Dutch
Caribbean possessions with the Netherlands. But these were the
exceptions. At the margin countries such as Algeria, although for
a long time virtually part of France, along with Portuguese Africa
claimed to be occupied territories with foreign minorities and all
eventually chose independence, not integration with their one-time
parent states.

It follows that the vast majority of these territories must be treated
as non-European dependencies within the context of colonialism;
and equally that the metropolitan powers were faced with the same
fundamental problems as Britain and France. To divide these states
into neat categories according to their approach to these problems
would be to distort complex realities, for each evolved its special
mix of techniques. There was, in fact, much common ground. All
except the USA had a central colonial ministry (under different
names) and all left the running of colonial matters to professional
administrators, both at home and in the colonies. Nowhere, except

in American possessions, were the inhabitants given a significant share in the process of government. The Netherlands came nearest to doing so by establishing a *Volksrad*, part nominated, part elected, in Indonesia in 1916; but even this had restricted powers analogous to a French *conseil de gouvernement*. Everywhere else government remained in the hands of officials appointed by the metropolis with virtually arbitrary powers, and the main variation lay in the character of the subordinate local administration. In this also the range of practices lay within the spectrum between direct and indirect rule as evolved by Britain and France for there was really no third option; and again practice varied immensely, even within individual empires and territories. Most powers made some attempt to preserve and work through those indigenous institutions that seemed most difficult to destroy or convenient to use. The Dutch long preserved sultans and other rulers in Indonesia while using indigenous 'regents' as bureaucrats in Java. The Germans adopted indirect rule on the Nigerian pattern in part of the Cameroons; and the Belgians, after they took responsibility for the Congo from Leopold II in 1908, also showed enthusiasm for this principle, though their system was essentially centralized and bureaucratic. Even the Italians collaborated with Islamic rulers in parts of Libya and Eritrea. On the whole, however, the dominant feature of all these colonial systems was direct rule on the French rather than indirect rule on the British pattern. The almost invariable result was that power was held by a small corps of European administrators who appointed indigenous subordinates to official posts and used these to control their territories. This implied a major and irretrievable break with the pre-colonial past and ensured that the new successor states of the post-colonial era would inherit highly centralized and basically autocratic systems of government. The attempts made by several colonial powers to introduce democratic practices after 1945 had little impact on this underlying reality.

3. The balance sheets of colonialism

The key to a correct evaluation of colonialism as an historical phenomenon is the point made earlier in this chapter. Colonialism was not a rational or planned condition. It was rather the product of a unique set of circumstances before and during the later nineteenth century that resulted unpredictably in the formal partition of much of the world between the great powers. Few of these, it was argued, had a coherent preconceived idea of what they would do with the territories they claimed or of the problems these would create. Colonial rule was thus a complex improvization and an ideology of empire was evolved to justify what it was found necessary to do. It is true that, in the course of meeting this challenge, many in the imperial states came to believe that colonialism was a rational and permanent condition and that it benefited both imperial state and dependency. It is even possible that the second of these assumptions was correct. But equally it might represent self-deception. In Chapter II of this book an attempt is made to assess the economic consequences of empire. Here it is proposed to review the two most common assertions made by the two parties to the imperial relationship: by the imperialists that alien rule was the only way in which these 'backward' countries could have been 'modernized'; by the colonial subjects that colonialism was not only unnecessary but positively harmful to their general political and social development.

i. Two views of colonial rule

Two main factors in conjunction determined the character of colonialism in any one place. These were, on the one hand, the character and aims of the imperialists and the resources they were prepared to put into their dependencies; on the other, the character of each dependent people and how they reacted to alien rule.

The characteristic common to most imperialists of all nationalities was that they believed that they had something of value to offer the peoples they ruled. In this they were supported by a quiverful of assumptions. Europeans would end slavery, suppress 'pagan' practices such as infanticide, introduce Christianity, cure disease, stop endemic warfare, provide education and economic development. They believed that they alone could do these things because they came from societies more advanced than those they ruled; and many believed that the white man was genetically superior to all others. They therefore justified alien rule on the ground that colonialism was a necessary instrument of 'modernization' which would help other peoples to do what they could not have done, or have done as well, by themselves. In so far as these objectives were pursued honestly they perhaps entitled the colonialists to rest with a good conscience.

Yet good intentions are not sufficient. On the imperial side the main defect of colonialism was that the administrators on the spot lacked both the tools and the qualifications to carry through their stated programmes. All modern colonies were starved of resources. No colony paid a money tribute to its parent state, but all were extremely poor because the tax-base in a less-developed country is very limited. Conversely metropolitan states, such as Britain, could not possibly have afforded the cost of large-scale permanent subsidies to so many dependencies, though grants in aid were common for limited periods and from 1929 additional funds were available under the Colonial Development Act. As a result all tropical colonies were run on a shoe-string. There were very few European administrators, doctors, engineers and other technicians. Education was usually done on the cheap by relying heavily on Christian missions, and this had important cultural and psychological consequences. Medical activities were largely restricted to tackling endemic disease. As for economic development, colonial governments could do little more than provide an infrastructure of communications and public utilities.

Those who ran the colonies seem also, in retrospect, to have been inadequately equipped intellectually. The quality and amount of training they received increased and improved over time as the first generation of soldier-administrators was replaced by civilians and institutions such as the French Ecole Coloniale were set up. Yet for the most part these men remained amateurs in most aspects of the problems with which they had to deal. Few had any real knowledge of the societies in which they were to work when they arrived there, though many became expert over time. Above all, perhaps, they were confused about their goals. Ironically this was less true in the early period after 1870 when the common assumption was that non-Europeans should be made as like Europeans as possible. The more this assumption was questioned on ethical and practical grounds the more uncertain men became of what they were trying to do and what the ultimate purpose of colonialism was. It is not surprising that most seem to have fallen back on a benevolently conservative paternalism, cultivating good relations with those under their control, adopting, chameleon-like, quasi-loyalties to the district, race or tribe with whom they worked and becoming hostile to proposals for innovation. Hubert Deschamps, who spent a lifetime administering parts of French Africa and Malagasy at all levels, and later became a professor of African history at the Sorbonne, subsequently summed up the typical attitude of the French colonial administrator before 1945 as follows:

> There was always the illusion of the virtue of compromise and of peaceful economic and social evolution during unlimited periods towards undefined political ends.... Like parents who refuse to see their children grow up, one administered from day to day without thinking about the evolution that one ought to be conducting. When maturity came in 1945 one would improvise in a whirlwind of eloquence and a vertigo of policy....[10]

These limitations were the direct and inevitable outcome of the attitude of all the imperial powers to their colonies: so long as these provided whatever advantages they looked for (strategic bases, raw materials, perhaps merely the satisfaction of imperial ownership), few cared anything about what happened to them or their inhabitants. Meantime most Europeans were confident that colonialism was in the best interests of their coloured subjects.

But from the standpoint of the one-time subject peoples (in so far as a European can judge their feelings) the case looks very different. Colonialism was unnecessary and what it did was damaging. Few people in any society welcome change imposed by others, though they may be glad to accept the same changes if these are adopted voluntarily. Many Africans, Asians and Pacific islanders admired much of what they knew of European civilization while they were still independent and invited various forms of collaboration which might help them to share these benefits. Hence, in retrospect, it is commonly claimed that these peoples could have absorbed all they wanted from Europe without formal subjugation. Empire may even have been counter-productive because it sometimes associated European civilization in people's minds with military conquest, destruction of social and religious systems, taxation, or forced labour. Similarly alien rule, by destroying or debilitating indigenous systems of government and patterns of authority, removed those in native society whose leadership was needed to promote change and thus made it more difficult for the colonial peoples to act for themselves. Subordination also bred a 'colonial mentality' that accepted inferior status and depended on aliens for leadership.

These things might have been more bearable had they been accompanied by a massive economic, social and educational advance; and it is a key element in the general indictment of colonialism that this compensation was not paid. On the contrary, so many have argued, the colonialists exploited their dependencies, taking out more wealth than they created and, in the end, creating 'underdevelopment', a condition in which all the mainsprings of economic and social development were cauterized because the imperial powers, or their nationals, came to control all the sources of wealth and applied these to their own ends rather than to the development of the colonies. In this way the colonial societies gained nothing from their subordination and were eventually discarded onto an historical waste-heap when the imperialists found it convenient to do so.

ii. The balance of probability

The key to resolving these apparently incompatible attitudes to colonialism lies in the premise underlying the anti-imperialist argument, that the non-European peoples could have gained all and more than they did fron contact with Europeans without formal occupation, and would have emerged stronger and more self-reliant as a result. The difficulty with this assumption is that, while there is no way of proving that it is untrue, there are few grounds for thinking that, in the course of natural development, any large proportion of the less-developed countries of the nineteenth-century world could or would have developed in this way if left alone. There are many reasons for thinking that the majority would have not been able or willing to adopt the more valuable products of western civilization – though these varied immensely from one geographical area to another – without undergoing the trauma of alien occupation. We can, in the first instance, separate off a number of countries which were certainly or probably capable of modernizing themselves and for whom alien rule, in the few instances that it took place, was irrelevant to progress: Japan, China, parts of South-east Asia, Turkey,

Egypt, Tunis, Iran; and, at the margin of probability, other Islamic states such as Morocco. Japan is, of course, the best example of a country that chose to 'go it alone' and emerged as an equal of the industrialized states of Europe and North America; though it must be remembered that the initial and perhaps necessary stimulus in this direction was given by the United States in the 1850s when Japan, like China a decade earlier, was forced to open her ports to foreign trade and accept direct communication with the West. All the other Asian countries were as resistant to foreign influence as Japan had been and even those that evaded formal colonial rule only opened their gates under naval or military pressure. Such pressures were imperialistic in that Europeans or Americans compelled other societies to join the international market and accept foreign influence against the will of xenophobic indigenous regimes. The results were not uniformly successful. None progressed as fast or as far as Japan because Japan possessed political and social institutions that were exceptionally, perhaps uniquely, adapted to modernization. Yet the examples of Turkey and Siam suggest that most of these countries might have done as well as they did whether or not they experienced colonial rule.

What all these places had in common was that they were more or less consolidated political units with relatively efficient and sophisticated systems of government, literate cultures and comparatively advanced economic structures, all of which were capable of being adapted to use new foreign techniques. This was not true of the majority of other territories that formed the bulk of modern colonial empires. However well they may have been adapted to their natural environment, very few if any of them appear to have possessed the capacity to act as modern nation states, adopting western technology as the basis for economic and social development. The obstacles varied in every place. In much of sub-Saharan Africa, for instance, political units were too small or were unstable; literacy was rare except in Islamic regions; existing social and economic systems were seldom well suited to modernization; communications were very primitive. This is not to deny that individuals or groups in Africa did or could show capacity to adopt European concepts and techniques and to respond to the opportunities of the international market. The pre-colonial history of West Africa in particular shows a very impressive response to new opportunities. What remains in doubt is how far such developments could have gone autonomously. It was one thing for West Africans to develop a large export/import trade by exploiting their natural endowment, exporting slaves, vegetable oil, ivory, etc.; but quite another for them to break through the technological and, above all, the political obstacles that would ultimately have put a limit on the volume and quality of their products. To go much beyond the levels reached by the 1880s would have required a fundamental restructuring and much investment, particularly in communications and methods of processing natural products. Could even a relatively powerful and enterprising state such as Dahomey have provided the political conditions necessary to attract foreign investment and stimulate indigenous production? How could the politically fragmented areas have dealt with disorder and intense local competition, as in the Niger Delta? Size is, in fact, very important. It is commonly and rightly said that most of the post-colonial states of West Africa, except possibly Nigeria, are too small in size, population and resources and too lacking in unity to constitute effective political or ecomonic units; yet all are immensely larger and more centralized than any indigenous state that was, or might have been, built up in the same time-period by African empire-builders, enterprising though many of these then were. If this is true of West Africa, it is far more true of almost all other areas of Africa. In political terms the only exception is Ethiopia, which escaped Italian rule in 1896 and was not occupied until 1935/6. Yet Ethiopia is not a good case in support of the proposition that indigenous states would have prospered if left alone. Despite its literacy and powerful central government, Ethiopia achieved virtually no economic development in those forty years.

It is, therefore, necessary to reformulate the alternative courses historically open to less-developed areas during the era after about 1870. If they had not become European possessions the majority would probably have remained very much as they were. A few, such as Egypt, which had been doing this for half a century, might have succeeded in importing foreign capital and technology and using these to develop the economy while preserving their independence and culture. In parts of West Africa small enclaves might have developed in which African entrepreneurs collaborated with foreign

merchants and capitalists to establish modern commercial enterprises under informal European political supervision. In most other
places the most likely development was that private foreign enterprise would have continued to penetrate local economic life, relying
precariously on political support from local rulers. It seems very unlikely that this penetration could have been checked by any except
the strongest or most inaccessible indigenous state; and all the available evidence of the decades before formal European rule was
imposed suggests that the damage such uncontrolled incursions were
likely to do to an indigenous society was very great. The one thing
that seems unlikely to have happened was that these states could
have retained control of events and have emerged as powerful prosperous societies independent of foreign capitalism.

iii. Conclusions: the place of colonialism in modern history

The logical outcome of these arguments is that colonialism, especially in tropical Africa and the Pacific, was historically the lesser of
two evils facing most indigenous peoples in the later nineteenth century. Alien rule is intrinsically inconsistent with liberal western
values; but there are worse things that can happen to any people.
In the nineteenth century the out-thrust of Europe and North
America was so strong and the capacity of most other societies to
resist or make constructive use of that force so limited, that the real-
istic alternative to formal imperial rule was widespread anarchy.
Many indigenous rulers recognized this clearly and invited foreign
'protection' to avert the danger, though some were later dis-
appointed to find that the price of protection was total subordination
or even removal. Colonialism was thus a virtually automatic reflex
on both sides of the relationship to acute problems of international
relations.

   If colonialism is seen in this way, rather than as a deliberately constructed system of international servitude, it is not surprising that
it should have been riddled with internal contradictions. On the one
hand it came to be seen as an unwanted burden for the imperialists
which a minority of optimists among them sought to turn to the
advantage of the metropolis by constructing schemes for imperial

economic development. On the other hand it came increasingly to be regarded by subject peoples, particularly by the growing number of western-educated intellectuals, who saw their own situation through liberal western eyes, as an intolerable affront to the dignity of their own people. Ultimately the twin forces of imperial disillusionment and moral concern and colonial resentment and ambition fused to generate decolonization. This was the dialectic of colonialism as an historical phenomenon. In its beginning was its end.

The tragedy, seen from the standpoint of the 1970s, is that the colonial period was for many countries too short for the historical process to reach maturity. If colonialism is seen as a holding operation during which the colonial territories could overcome the structural problems that had made alien rule possible and even necessary, that operation was far from complete in most countries by the time of decolonization. This was not so everywhere. Where alien rule had been least necessary at the start (that is, where it was not the result of acute crisis in the indigenous society or where native systems of government were most efficient) and where colonial rule had been in operation for a long period, decolonization often came too late. India, Ceylon, Indonesia, possibly Indo-China, Burma and other countries were as well prepared psychologically and institutionally for sovereign independence some decades before they achieved it as they were after 1945. But in most other colonial territories the process of homogenizing relatively small ethnic and political groups into proto-nation states had hardly begun by 1945 and was almost everywhere incomplete by the date of independence. The blame can be apportioned at will. The imperialists, it has been argued, lacked clear long-term objectives, were too conservative and put too little into their possessions. Had they planned to create new sovereign states earlier on they might well have done so more successfully. For their part indigenous politicians demanded the power that freedom would give them before their countries were ready for it. In the event it is they who pay the price. Wherever the blame lies, the one fundamental truth about European colonialism is that it was from the start an unstable and transient condition, the product of a particular conjunction in world history which disappeared as surely as spring succeeds winter.

Notes

1. In *Imperialism, the Highest Stage of Capitalism*, (1916, English edition Moscow 1947), pp. 91–2.

2. See J.A. Schumpeter, *Imperialism and Social Classes*, (1919, English edition Oxford 1951).

3. Franz Fanon, *The Wretched of the Earth*, (English edition New York 1966).

4. C. Furtado, *Development and Underdevelopment*, (California 1964).

5. Schumpeter, op. cit., p. 7.

6. He summarized these in his book, *La Mise en Valeur des Colonies françaises* (Paris 1923).

7. D.K. Fieldhouse, *The Colonial Empires* (London 1966).

8. Lugard set out his ideas most fully in *The Dual Mandate in British Tropical Africa*, (London 1922 3rd ed. London 1926).

9. Quoted in S.H. Roberts, *History of French Colonial Policy, 1870–1925* (2 vols London 1925), Vol I, p. 113.

10. 'French Policy in Africa between the Wars' in *France and Britain in Africa*, ed. P.G. Gifford and W.R. Louis (New Haven Conn. 1971), pp. 568–9.

II. The Economics of Colonialism

1. The issues

It has long been conventional to believe that colonialism was primarily a device by which the rich imperial states could exploit their dependencies and, consequentially, that the effect of colonialism was to perpetuate, or even to create, poverty in the colonies. These beliefs stretch back at least to the eighteenth century, when the early economists, such as Adam Smith, denounced the colonial economic systems of their day on the ground that, as Smith put it in his *The Wealth of Nations*, regulation of the economic life of the colonies by the metropolitan states 'tends to diminish, or, at least, to keep down below what they would otherwise rise to, both the enjoyments and industry of all these nations in general, and of the American colonies in particular'.[1] Marx, although he did not develop the theme, believed that advanced countries could obtain a better return on their capital by investing in colonies 'for the simple reason that the rate of profit is higher there on account of the backward development, and for the added reason, that slaves, coolies, etc., permit a better exploitation of labour'.[2] Thereafter belief that empire was intended to exploit is reflected in all radical and socialist writing on colonialism, leading to the extreme position adopted by contemporary 'underdevelopment' theorists who argue that alien rule did not merely fail to develop colonial societies but actually made them 'poor' and destroyed their inherent capacity to develop successfully. Thus Walter Rodney concluded in his book *How Europe Underdeveloped Africa* that under colonialism 'the only things that developed were dependency and underdevelopment'.[3]

Such allegations have not gone unchallenged, Parallel with those who denounced colonialism there have always been others who claimed that it was a means whereby the more developed imperial states could and did transmit their own more advanced institutions and technology to less-developed regions. Many, indeed, held that this was a moral obligation. Thus Lord Lugard in his book *The Dual Mandate in British Tropical Africa*, first published in 1922, argued that 'Our present task is clear. It is to promote the commercial and industrial progress of Africa, without too careful a scrutiny of the material gains to ourselves.'[4] This belief became characteristic of the rhetoric of European imperialists from then until the age of decolonization after 1945. It gave them a good conscience and was expressed after the Second World War in grandiose schemes for public investment and vast programmes of international aid.

There are, therefore, two incompatible assessments of the economic consequences of modern colonialism. Either may be correct, but equally the truth may lie between these poles. It is the aim of this chapter to survey some of the evidence and to suggest where the balance of probability appears to lie. But it must be said at the start that, in the nature of such large questions, no firm conclusions can be reached. The difficulty is that, in attempting to assess the economic impact of alien rule, both historians and economists lack a firm basis in fact. Those pessimists who claim that empire was destructive lack reliable information on the social and economic conditions of pre-colonial societies. No one knows, or can accurately estimate, the population, production or incomes of African or Asian countries in the nineteenth century before they became colonies. As late as the 1950s statistics on most African dependencies are largely guess-work. Critics of colonialism such as Rodney, and even the very scholarly Marxist historian of French West Africa, Jean Suret-Canale,[5] make very favourable inferences on pre-colonial conditions from dubious evidence; and on this shaky foundation construct counter-factual propositions to suggest that, if left alone, these non-European societies might have developed far more successfully than they did under colonial conditions. Conversely those who believe in the beneficial effects of empire have tended to accept too uncritically the very adverse comments made by many early European explorers, missionaries and others who, because they judged too narrowly by European standards, saw only poverty, inefficiency and stagnation in societies which may, in relation to their environment, have been comparatively efficient and able to respond to new external stimuli. Either way a distorted view of the economic consequences of European rule is certain to result.

It is, therefore, wise to limit our objectives. If we cannot accurately measure progress or regress because there are no certain benchmarks at either end of the historical time-span, it is at least possible to analyse some of the characteristic features of colonialism as they are likely to have affected economic development. The first need is to discover what practical difference empire made in economic terms, and this involves examination of the basic features of an imperial economy. The second is to look at the actual performance of colonial economies to see what effects the system of imperial controls had on their development. For reasons already outlined this cannot be done with any precision and it would be impossible here to deal in detail with all the vast number of colonial territories. It is therefore proposed to concentrate on two basic issues – specialization in agricultural production for export and limited industrialization – which have often been regarded as symptomatic of colonialism, and to draw evidence mainly from three large colonial territories – British India, French West Africa and the Belgian Congo – which between them typify a wide range of divergent problems, policies and developments.

2. The character of an imperial economy

By far the most important feature of colonialism as it affected the economic life of any dependency was the simple fact that government, and therefore economic management, were in alien hands. The point may seem too obvious to state; yet it was this, rather than any specific aspects of economic organization or policy, that differentiated a colony from an independent state. It was for this reason that President Nkrumah of Ghana later advised his fellow Africans still under colonial rule that they should seek first the political kingdom. Equally it was political control that differentiated colonialism from what is often described as 'neo-colonialism' after formal imperial rule was withdrawn. Control of government gave the imperial states the power, if they chose to use it, of moulding the economic life of the colonies in whatever way they chose or, alternatively, of allowing 'natural' economic forces to operate freely. Either way the imperial power was bound to lay down the rules within which colonial economic life operated. Each state adopted different policies but all faced similar problems. Their responses fall into two general categories: external regulations concerning the relations between the colony and the rest of the world, of which tariffs and monetary policy were the most important; and internal policies specific to individual colonies on questions such as land usage, labour and governmental intervention in economic affairs. These will be examined in turn.

i. External regulations

a. Tariffs

Conventionally tariffs, along with physical controls on trade, have always been regarded as the most important constituent of imperial economic policies. Probably this is correct because most less-developed countries depend heavily on their import/export trade and, by fixing the terms on which this trade was conducted, the colonial powers could significantly affect the performance of the colonial economy and its relations with the metropolis.

Historically the primary aim of all the European states was to use commercial regulations to maximize their share of colonial trade in both directions and the profits they made from it. Before the mid-nineteenth century physical controls were more important than tariffs in achieving these objects. The English navigation acts, dating from the 1650s, on which Adam Smith based his analysis of what he described as 'mercantilism', may be taken as typical, though they were in fact more liberal than the rules enforced by most other states. All colonial trade must be carried in British-owned and registered ships. All goods imported to the colonies must either be the product of Britain or be transhipped and pay duties there. Any colonial exports so 'enumerated' must be carried direct to a British port in the first instance. The aim of these rules was, of course, to give British shipowners, merchants and manufacturers an assured benefit from colonial commerce and to enable the government to tax colonial trade. In addition the colonies were forbidden to manufacture or to export a limited range of products. These physical controls were buttressed by a system of preferential tariffs. Many British exports paid lower duties on entering the colonies than did foreign goods, and some colonial products, notably sugar, had an advantage over goods entering Britain from foreign countries. This implied that the 'old colonial system' was not entirely one-sided; and in addition a range of colonial products which the British wished to stimulate attracted bounties (subsidies) when sold in Britain.

Such devices were common to all the imperial systems until the 1820s; but thereafter large differences developed. As the first industrialized country, Britain saw that she no longer needed to protect her home manufacturers or her colonial trade and also that she now stood to benefit from universal abolition of both physical controls and protective tariffs. By the 1850s Britain therefore abolished these restrictions, so that from then until 1932 (when she adopted a general protective tariff at home and established preferential tariffs throughout most of her empire) the British empire was free trading. The effect was that Britain and the colonies were open to the ships and goods of all countries on precisely equal terms and also that no import duty that was imposed to raise public revenue should also provide protection for local producers. In some places this last principle was carried to dogmatic extremes. In India import duties on cotton cloths were abolished in 1879. In 1893 a 5 per cent import duty was imposed to offset a shortfall in revenue resulting from the decline in the value of the silver currency and this produced an outcry from the Lancashire cotton manufacturers on the ground that it provided protection for Indian cotton manufacturers. Under pressure from London the Indian government then reluctantly placed a 5 per cent excise duty on cotton goods made in India and thereafter import duty and excise were kept in balance until after 1923, when India was given freedom to establish protective duties. Similar principles lasted much longer in other British colonies. To take a single example, to the day of its independence in 1957 the Gold Coast (Ghana) had an import duty on the raw materials needed to manufacture soap which balanced the duty paid on imported soap. The result was that there was absolutely no incentive for any African entrepreneur or foreign company to manufacture soap there until the government of Ghana abolished the import duty on raw materials and raised that on imported soap in the early 1960s.

The British hoped that the rest of the imperial powers would follow their example, and up to a point they did. The Dutch and

Belgians adopted free trade in full at home and in their colonies. The French, Portuguese and Spanish relaxed physical controls on colonial trade and shipping, and neither the Germans nor the Americans, when these states acquired colonies late in the nineteenth century, attempted to exclude foreign ships or goods. Yet none of these states adopted free trade in full and by the early twentieth century they had created protectionist systems which, as they affected their colonies, have often been described as 'neo-mercantilist'. The French case may be taken as typical, though in fact each was different. French protective tariffs began to rise in 1881 and reached a climax with the Méline tariff of 1892. Simultaneously the aim was to assimilate the colonial tariff as closely as possible to that of the metropolis, though this was not possible in all cases since international treaties forbade preferential duties in parts of French West and Equatorial Africa, Tunis and Morocco. The result was to give French exporters a substantial advantage over foreign competitors in most of the colonies, though colonial producers had no protection against products of France. Most other colonial powers followed this example, either incorporating their colonies within the metropolitan tariff or giving their own goods preferential treatment in their dependencies. Such policies were clearly in the interest of the metropolis and against that of a colony. But from the 1930s, when primary producing countries faced economic crisis, France went one stage further and adopted a system of support prices for certain primary commodities from her colonies when sold in France. This was achieved by imposing high specific duties on the same goods coming from foreign countries, coupled with quotas which guaranteed French colonial producers a share of the French market. This system lasted until 1939, was revived after 1945 and, in modified form, became an integral part of the European Economic Community in 1958.

There were, therefore, two contrasting patterns of tariff policy in the modern period; and, although the distinction was blurred after 1932, when the British adopted protection at home and preferences in many of the colonies, its significance for the colonies was very considerable. First, although tariff preferences did not necessarily ensure a monopoly of a colonial market for the metropolitan exporter, the effect of the tariff, institutional links through business houses, etc., the predominance of national shipping lines, which were often given subsidies by the state, and political pressures tended collectively to raise the proportion of intra-imperial trade well above the level likely to have existed if a dependency had been politically free. Thus the French share of total imports to French West Africa rose from 36.4 per cent in 1920 to 69 per cent in 1939; whereas Britain's share of imports to her free-trading West African colonies declined from 79.2 per cent in 1920 to 46.3 per cent in 1947. This no doubt benefited French manufacturers; but since consumers in Francophone Africa had to pay far more for their imports than they would under free trade conditions, the result was to raise general price levels in French colonies well above those in other places, which in turn made French colonial exports less competitive. Hence the need for a guaranteed market in France. At the same time, of course, the French system acted as a forcing house to stimulate production of agricultural exports to the protected metropolitan market and this may have contributed to the rapid growth of the more favoured colonies, such as the Ivory Coast.

Free trade was good for colonial consumers and French price supports for commodity exports to the metropolis helped colonial primary producers; but neither stimulated investment in local manufacture in the colonies, and this has been one of the main indictments against both types of imperial economic management. The problem of industrialization can, in fact, be seen in either of two ways. From a free trade standpoint, one of whose basic principles as defined by David Ricardo was the pursuit of 'comparative advantage', each society should produce only those things which it could make or grow at least as cheaply as it could import them since this ensured the most efficient use of resources by all countries. If a small and poor colony could not support local manufacturing because local industries could not compete in an open market against products imported from established industrial countries, that colony should accept the fact and concentrate on other forms of production. Conversely, if, as happened in India, industry developed on a large scale under free trade conditions, this proved that that country possessed the necessary factor endowment for industrialization (raw materials, adequate labour force, capital, know-how and a sufficient market) and these industries were likely to prove durable and socially profitable. This was the conventional British view of the matter until at least the 1920s.

But there was an alternative approach to the same situation. As Friedrich List, the Prussian economist, pointed out in his *National System of Political Economy*, published in 1841, free trade ignored the fact that many potential industrial ventures, which might thrive once firmly established, could never overcome their early problems without protection. Any new industrial venture, particularly in a less-developed country, was relatively inefficient at the start. An entrepreneur might lack know-how and have limited capital. He had no trained labour force to call on and initially he had to sell his products to consumers habituated to foreign imported goods and who probably believed that local products were inferior. Above all, his sales volume would be restricted to a local market which was commonly too small to provide economies of scale. To accept these obstacles as insuperable condemned all countries, except those that had industrialized first, to perpetual dependence on agriculture. The better alternative was for a less-developed country to accept that industrialization entailed temporary hardship to consumers and to impose import duties to protect what came to be called 'infant industries' until they could stand on their own feet, after which the protective shield should be removed.

This argument convinced many then and later, including John Stuart Mill, who remained convinced of the essential rightness of the free trade position. They did so, however, only on the assumption that duties imposed to protect infant industries were temporary, for otherwise the consumer would be saddled indefinitely with protected industries which had no incentive to increase their efficiency. Thus it was that when, in 1923, the British took one of the most important steps in the history of modern colonialism and set up a Tariff Board in India with power to recommend the creation of protective duties there, even against British imports, it was supposed to apply the following three criteria to all applications for protection. First, that India possessed natural advantages for that industry. Second, that the industry was unlikely to develop without protection because of foreign competition. Third, that in the end the industry was likely to be able to operate at a profit without tariff protection. These principles were impeccable and were applied rigorously during the 1920s. The problem in India, as in all newly industrializing countries, was, of course, that once a new industry had become accustomed to a given level of protection, its owners were likely to oppose any reduction of the import tariff because this would reduce their profit margins or even demonstrate that they were incapable of competing on an open market. Later developments in India and elsewhere suggest that those austere free traders who rejected the infant industry principle on these grounds may have been right. Under slump conditions these three principles ceased to be applied in India, industry became accustomed to very heavy protection, and by 1961 the effective protection provided there by import duties and import restrictions combined amounted to 313 per cent on one-sixth of large-scale manufacturing enterprises. In Pakistan two years later the average for all manufactures was 271 per cent,[6] and comparable developments have occurred in many less-developed countries since 1945. Ultimately, of course, the price of allowing a weak infant industry to become a perpetual convalescent is paid by the domestic consumer.

This suggests that there may have been a much stronger case than is often allowed for the rigorous free trade principles enforced by the British, Dutch and Belgians on their colonial possessions: at least consumers in these countries could buy goods, whether imported or locally produced, at strictly competitive prices. The same cannot be said of the inhabitants of French, Portuguese, Spanish, Italian and American possessions who were subject to a double disability. On the one hand local manufacturing was discouraged by the fact that products from the parent states had free or virtually free entry, so that local entrepreneurs faced the same difficulties in meeting competition from established imports as those in free trade colonies. On the other hand, since imports coming from outside the particular imperial system were subject to discriminating duties, the colonial consumer found himself paying a price inflated by these duties. As a result the colonial subjects of France and other protectionist countries suffered both from lack of local industrialization and from high prices, and these disabilities were offset only to the extent that each metropolitan country provided a protected market for quotas of colonial primary products at premium prices.

Clearly tariffs had a major formative influence on the economic development of modern colonial economies. In the literature on colonialism their use by the imperial authorities has conventionally been criticized on the grounds that they sacrified the interests of the dependent peoples to those of the imperialists. This may have been so, at least to the extent that special interest groups in the metropolitan countries, such as the Lancashire cotton manufacturers, were responsible for particular policies. Yet three reservations must be made. First, many free traders genuinely believed that an 'open door' was in the best long-term interests of the colonies. Second, it is very unlikely that many of these countries, even had they not become dependencies, could have resisted foreign pressure to maintain very low tariffs. China and the Ottoman empire, for example, were forced by what the Chinese called the 'unequal treaties' to keep tariffs very low and to provide special facilities to foreign merchants. Finally, it remains extremely doubtful whether intensive protection is at any time in the best interests of less-developed countries. With sufficient protection almost any country can stimulate foreign or indigenous capitalists to invest in local manufacture of almost anything. But, as economists have at all times pointed out, no benefit and probably much harm accrues to a country that does this unless it genuinely possesses the potential to manufacture efficiently in the long run. The record of many new ex-colonial states since 1945 suggests that few have escaped this danger. Conversely three countries that had an outstanding record of industrial growth – Taiwan, South Korea and Hong Kong – were all free trading so far as their export industries were concerned. The conclusion is not that imperial tariff policy was necessarily the best for the colonies but that it was not wrong merely because it did not deliberately stimulate their industrialization. In Part 3 of this chapter a more detailed examination will be made of conditions favouring and obstructing industrialization in three large colonial possessions.

b. *Monetary policy*
Imperial policy on currency and monetary systems had basically the same objectives as tariff policy in that its primary function was to facilitate economic relations between metropolis and colony. This could be done in either of two ways. Colonies could be given the same currency as the metropolis or they could have a separate

currency pegged to that of the metropolis at an appropriate rate of exchange. The particular means mattered less than the general effect; but provision of an imperial monetary system was bound to have a very important influence on the evolution of the colonial economy.

The starting point of all imperial monetary policies was the assumption that empires were units which should have uniform institutions wherever possible. The simplest way of doing this was to impose the metropolitan currency, including its coins, on each dependency. This was sometimes done, for example, by the Belgians in the Congo and the Dutch in Indonesia. But there were three obstacles to doing this universally. First, European denominations were not necessarily suited to the needs of very poor communities which needed coins representing very small values. Second, so long as coins had intrinsic metallic value and colonial paper money was not legal tender, it was necessary to transport large amounts of coin to settle balance of payment accounts. Third, many of the more advanced European possessions, particularly those in North Africa and Asia, had their own pre-colonial currencies which it would have been pointless and difficult to replace. For these and other reasons the British and French, with the largest imperial systems, came to recognize that effective unity could best be achieved by a system of local colonial currencies, each tied to that of the metropolis and fully convertible, rather than by a uniform system. Even so the attempt by each power to maintain fixed parities and full convertibility throughout its empire created problems and raised important issues concerning economic relations under colonialism.

For the British the first and most important question was what relationship to establish between the silver-based Indian rupee and the gold-based British pound.[7] Until 1893 the rupee was an independent currency whose rate of exchange with the pound was fixed from time to time by the British government according to the price of silver but was usually about Rs. 1 = 2/- sterling. In the early 1890s, however, the value of silver dropped and in 1893 the rupee had to be called down to Rs. 1 = 1/4d. Since this amounted to devaluation it was good for Indian exports and industry, but made it difficult for the Indian government to service its overseas liabilities and reduced the sterling value of profits, savings, etc. made by British nationals in India. The new ratio was nevertheless maintained by monetary management until the First World War, when an appreciation in the price of silver and the devaluation of the pound resulted in revaluation of the rupee to 2/– in 1920. But the price of silver then dropped quickly and the exchange rate with the pound fluctuated until the rupee was down to 1/4d.

This instability in the rates of exchange between two currencies within a single empire was extremely inconvenient, given the close economic and financial relationships between Britain and India, and made it necessary for the first time to consider first principles of currency management. An official investigation was held and in 1927 it was decided to ignore metallic values and to tie the rupee to the pound at Rs. 1 = 1/6d. The result was an outcry that demonstrated the political difficulties inherent in decisions of this type. Indian nationalists complained bitterly that the rupee was now overvalued, that this rate was fixed to benefit British interests (holders of Indian government stock, Indian based companies, civil servants, etc.) and that conversely it was bad for India because it made Indian products uncompetitive overseas and helped British exporters to compete in the Indian market. This was probably the first time since the 1760s that British imperial monetary policy had received such intense criticism in a dependency (though the devaluation of the 1890s had been criticized by some Indians) and it indicated that in the new era of managed currencies such issues could endanger imperial relationships. In the event, however, the 1927 rupee exchange rate proved viable. It lasted until after the British devaluation of 1949 and was no longer a matter of controversy. Yet this episode served notice that once currencies had ceased to be based on intrinsic metallic value and were managed by the imperial authorities, monetary policy was likely to become a major source of friction between metropolis and colony. This became evident by the early 1940s in the case of the African colonies, though these had an entirely different type of currency.

What distinguished all sub-Saharan European possessions in Africa from those in Asia was that none possessed currencies comparable with those of Europe. During the first phase of colonial rule, therefore, Britain, in common with France, gradually injected metropolitan coins into these new colonies. For many reasons, however, it seemed more desirable that these and other groups of colonies should have their own coinage; and from 1912 the British therefore created a number of regional monetary systems (West Africa, East Africa, Palestine, Central Africa and the West Indies) each of which was autonomous but was regulated by a Currency Board in Britain. The basic principle of the Colonial Sterling Exchange Standard, as it came to be called, was that the coinage was specific to each area and so could not be exported, but that each was fully convertible into sterling at face value and thence into foreign currencies. Initially the system was uncontroversial because the colonial silver coins possessed the same intrinsic value as British coins, so that no issues arose concerning rates of exchange or cover. But after 1920 the adoption of a fiduciary currency by Britain and the consequential devaluation of sterling raised difficult questions. The colonies, like Britain, now had token nickel coins and this made it necessary to arrange cover and fix exchange rates. British policy was to insist on 100 per cent cover, held in Britain in the form of British gilt-edged securities and bullion, and to maintain parity with the pound sterling. Both policies then became a matter of debate.

So far as the cover was concerned the criticism, formulated by British economists in the early 1940s and taken up by colonial nationalists, was that it was unreasonable to require a colony to maintain 100 per cent cover when Britain herself no longer did so. This requirement, it was held, had an adverse effect on colonial economic development. The colonial assets frozen in London as cover could have been put to better use if realized and invested in the colonies. More important, the money supply could not be used as a tool of economic management. It could only be expanded by buying additional coinage with export credits; and at a time of depression, when Keynesian theory required the creation of additional credit, the money supply was likely to be reduced by the need to sell colonial assets in London to balance a trade deficit. In short, the colonial currency system now seemed a tool of British imperial exploitation and nationalists demanded that each colony should have its own currency system and central bank as a means of furthering its own economic development.

By the 1940s, moreover, nationalists had an additional grievance. From 1939, to meet Britain's need for hard currency to pay for war supplies from America, all foreign exchange earnings made by countries within the sterling area (which included the whole empire except Canada and Newfoundland) had to be paid into a common pool, the Exchange Equalization Account, in London; and purchases from non-sterling countries required permission from the British authorities. Because Britain continued to run a balance of payments deficit after 1945 these restrictions were continued in a less extreme form (except for a short period of free convertibility under American pressure in 1947) until 1958. During this period the colonies were thus forced to build up sterling balances in London, which they could not even use freely to buy British goods because of the shortage of products available for export. The effect was that the colonies were forced to give Britain credit at low rates of interest at a time when their own economies were badly in need of capital goods for development purposes and consumer goods to damp down demand-led inflation.

The general significance of these British monetary policies for colonial economic development is very considerable, particularly when viewed from the vantage point of the post-decolonization period. On the credit side their main achievement was to ensure stable and, until 1939, fully convertible currencies in territories which had not previously possessed modern currencies, whose economies were too small and weak to sustain international confidence in an autonomous currency and whose governments, whether independent or colonial, lacked the sophistication to manage currency matters efficiently. Stability, convertibility and freedom to transfer assets encouraged overseas investors and at the same time ensured that the colonial economies remained competitive as part of an international market economy. Most of these advantages were lost when, after independence, the new states simultaneously adopted autonomous currencies and managed economies, resulting commonly in inflation and the end of convertibility. On the other hand it is arguable that well before 1945 the whole system of fixed parities between currencies within the British empire and the methods used to support the Colonial Sterling Exchange Standard had become vulnerable to criticism on three grounds. Fixed parities were not necessarily in the best interests of the colonies once the international value of the pound was manipulated to serve British rather than colonial interests. The need to maintain 100 per cent cover for colonial currencies was likely to have a deflationary effect on colonial economic growth. Finally, as Britain declined in relation to other developed countries, it was no longer desirable for the colonies to be as closely tied to the British economy as the imperial currency system tied them. On balance it would be reasonable to conclude that the British imperial monetary system served its purposes well enough down to 1939 but that thereafter the expanding economic needs of the dependencies demanded much greater flexibility. Ultimately decolonization and the fragmentation of the sterling area achieved this result.

It is impossible here to survey in comparable detail the monetary policies of the other imperial systems. Almost all, and particularly the Dutch in Indonesia, the Belgians in the Congo, the Italians in North and North-east Africa, the Portuguese in Africa and the Americans in their overseas territories, maintained their own identical and fully convertible currencies in the colonies, thus greatly strengthening the economic unity of their empires. But a brief mention must be made of France, owner of the second largest colonial empire, which adopted slightly different monetary policies both from these states and also from Britain.

Until 1930 France adopted one of two alternative policies in her overseas possessions. In the great majority she imposed the metropolitan franc, using standard French coins but allowing a single bank of issue in each territory or group to provide paper currency which, by contrast with practice in British territories, was legal tender. In Indo-China, however, which did not initially possess an indigenous currency comparable with that of India, France established an autonomous currency based on a silver piastre; and, despite recurrent demands by vested interests at home and in Indo-China that the piastre should be pegged to the franc as the rupee was pegged to the pound after 1893, the piastre was allowed, within limits, to fluctuate with the market value of silver. But in 1930 the piastre was at last pegged to the stabilized gold franc of 1928; and even when France devalued the franc in relation to gold in 1938, the piastre retained its parity with the franc.

At this point, therefore, French practice was close to that of

Britain and for the same reasons. From 1939, however, it changed substantially. After the defeat of France in 1940 central control of French colonial currency became impossible. From 1941 the currencies of those French territories under The Free French were pegged to the pound sterling at different rates of exchange according to local circumstances; and, although these were briefly integrated in 1944, this proved impossible to sustain. By the later 1940s, in addition to the metropolitan franc, which was in use in North Africa and the Caribbean, there was a separate CFA franc for tropical territories, a CPA franc for the Pacific possessions, the piastre for Indo-China and, from 1948, yet another franc for French Somali; and on each occasion that the metropolitan franc had to be devalued separate decisions were taken for each of these colonial currencies in the light of local circumstances. This system provided an essential element of flexibility in the French imperial currency system at a time of rapid inflation in France. But it is significant of the revived French interest in the economic unity of the empire that in 1949 all French colonial currencies were once again pegged to the metropolitan franc at the existing parities and that thereafter they moved up and down with it until the end of the colonial period. At the same time France evolved a much more liberal system for supporting colonial currencies which gave them full security and ensured convertibility without the rigorous restrictions imposed by the British. An important outcome was that the majority of Francophone African states after independence chose to retain their close monetary links with France whereas the ex-British territories chose monetary autonomy.

ii. Internal control of the colonial economy

Imperial tariff and monetary policies had a very great impact on the economic development of modern European colonies. Equally important was the character of the government within each dependency and the policies it adopted on specific economic and social issues; and, although it would be impossible to give a detailed account of these in the multitude of modern colonies, it is necessary to make some broad generalizations concerning the main fields of government activity, particularly in British and French possessions, since it is here that one might expect practice under a colonial regime to differ very obviously from that under a sovereign successor state.

a. The character of colonial government and the 'open economy'
Although they differed widely, the local governments of all colonies inevitably had an immense effect on the evolution of the colonial economies. The general character of these governments has been described in Chapter I. Here it is necessary only to emphasize certain features as they affected colonial economic life.

Seen positively, an obvious feature of colonial governments was that, being bureaucratic, they were relatively immune to popular pressures, consistent in the policies they adopted and law-abiding in their procedures. No general election or the needs of electioneering could deflect their course of action. Being mostly expatriates, officials were unconnected with local commercial activities and could take a neutral view of local claimants for favours. No one has yet demonstrated corruption at the higher levels of modern colonial government, though some have alleged that the hope of appointment to senior positions in large expatriate enterprises after retirement (such as the Union Minière in the Congo) may have influenced the attitudes of officials to these enterprises while holding public office. Thus, however dictatorial such governments might appear to colonial subjects, they embodied the concept of the rule of law and of government in the general interest, as officialdom interpreted this.

The negative aspect of this type of government, at least down to 1945, was that colonial officials did not believe in 'management' of the economy and relied on elementary fiscal measures to provide a basis for self-propelled economic growth. The conventional view was that, in addition to maintaining law and order, the main economic function of the state was to build the infrastructure of economic and social life to the limits of the ability of a particular colony to pay for emenities. Top priority was normally given to communications – railways, harbours, telegraphs, rivers and roads – since it was believed that these were the prerequisites of a modern economy, making it possible to link internal areas of production to the world commodity market. Second priority was given to power and water supplies, and to social services: education (mostly primary and health (particularly the eradication of endemic diseases).

Although by later criteria these priorities may seem to reflect an unduly narrow view of the economic and social functions of the state, it must be emphasized that in their context they represented a great extension of the contemporary functions of the state in Europe and North America. Before 1945, for example, none of the rail or canal systems of Britain were publicly owned and there was no national health service; whereas in sub-Saharan Africa the only privately owned railways in British territories were in the Rhodesias and Nyasaland and all non-self-governing colonies had government-operated medical services. Indeed it can be argued that state socialism of a type existed in British and French colonies long before it was introduced at home.

The fact nevertheless remains that the only area of production in which colonial governments took an active part was agriculture, which formed the basis of all tropical economies, provided the mainstay of the export trade and thus paid for the imports on which duties could be imposed to meet the costs of government. Most colonies had agricultural departments which maintained research establishments to experiment with improved strains of plants and trees and attempted to educate indigenous producers to use improved methods. These activities had considerable success and made it possible for most colonies to expand agricultural production to keep pace with international demand and rising population. Yet industrial production was virtually ignored. Probably no colonial government had a department of industry before 1945. The state almost never actively encouraged indigenous entrepreneurs to invest in local import-substituting industrial production. The government did not provide medium or long-term loans to help would-be capitalists, though the banking system, owned by banks in the metropolis and geared to the needs of the import/export trade, was seldom willing to provide these essential credit facilities to non-Europeans. There were very few technical schools capable of training men to become managers or businessmen. Apart from the Belgian Congo, where the state had shares in many industrial and commercial ventures, colonial governments almost never took the initiative in establishing or investing in industry. In short, the duty of government was to keep the peace, not to stimulate industrial development or indigenous enterprise.

The reasons for this negative attitude, for which colonialism has since been generally condemned, are complex. Until the 1930s governments in the metropolitan states did not expect to stimulate or take part in industry except by conventional management of money supply and tariffs. The underlying ideology of empire, based on belief that colonies should be complementary to the metropolis, was against artificial stimulation of industry in the dependencies. Colonial officials seldom came from industrial or commercial backgrounds and tended to despise these activities as ungentlemanly. Except in southern Asia, there were few indigenous entrepreneurs to put pressure on the government to provide support. Above all it was believed that economic forces must be allowed full play and that to strain against 'natural' obstacles to industrialization was inconsistent with the best interests of the colonial society for which the imperial authorities were trustees.

The general character of colonial government before 1945 (after which it changed fast and far in most dependencies) was thus to be reasonably efficient, impartial, incorrupt and non-interventionist. The economic outcome was the 'open economy' in which individuals, whether expatriate or indigenous, were left to pursue their own economic goals. The exceptions were few and generally unsuccessful in economic terms, notably the intensive state-settlement projects undertaken by the Italians in Libya and the Horn of Africa in the 1920s and 1930s, which cost the Italian taxpayer very dear and had disproportionately small results.[8]

b. Colonial policy on labour and land

In two fields colonial governments did intervene in economic and social life because experience showed that under the conditions of less-developed countries failure to act inhibited economic development. Since state action to ensure that land and labour were available to productive enterprises has often been regarded as a characteristic defect of colonialism it is necessary to consider why almost all colonial governments regarded this as a justifiable exception to their general non-interventionist approach.

There has been a common but misleading assumption, shared by most left-wing critics of colonialism from Marx onwards, that the main economic attraction of the colonies to European capitalists was that, by contrast with Europe, both land and labour were freely available (and therefore 'cheap') there and that this made it possible to generate 'super-profit'. The reality was different: indeed it is broadly true that where ample labour was available 'vacant' land was in relatively short supply; and conversely that where there was ample land, there was a limited supply of labour willing to work for Europeans or produce goods for European trade. European governments and entrepreneurs had, therefore, to adopt policies appropriate to the particular 'mix' of conditions in a particular place. Although there was an almost infinite gradation between different policies, three may be chosen as models: first, where there was a substantial population willing to produce on their own land for the market; second, where there was ample underutilized land but a shortage of willing workers; third, where there was a substantial group of European permanent settlers who wanted to operate farms, etc., but who found that both labour and land were in short supply.

The first of these patterns was most common in South and Southeast Asia. In places such as India and Java there were very limited opportunities for large-scale European land use, so the obvious policy was to stimulate the inhabitants to produce goods for the market on their own land. Fortunately for European merchants these peoples were commonly willing to respond to market stimuli to produce large quantities of cash crops such as sugar, jute, cotton, tobacco, etc. for export. This situation was not specific to colonialism and was little changed later by colonial independence. But there were variants on this situation where the imperial factor might be important. In the mid-nineteenth century the Dutch in Java used the so-called 'culture system' to compel Javanese peasants to allocate a certain proportion of their land and labour to produce export crops for the government in lieu of taxes. This system was wound up from the 1870s because it was considered an affront to the then dominant liberal economic theory, but the obligation to pay taxes in cash continued to provide an incentive for peasant farmers to grow marketable crops. The use of taxes to stimulate production then became almost universal in other colonies, particularly West Africa where African peasants already produced marketable commodities such as palm oil and ground-nuts. Where taxes alone were not sufficient, administrative pressures were often used to compel production of commodities which might not give the peasant as good a return as he might have obtained by concentrating on growing food for local consumption.

This combination of a relatively large labour force and the desire to produce for the market was, however, rare in tropical Africa, the Pacific and parts of southern Asia. In most places Europeans anxious to use the natural endowment for agriculture, mining, timber extraction, etc. commonly faced the obstacle that the population was not accustomed to growing or extracting these things on its own account on a commercial scale and was also reluctant to take paid work on the conditions offered by expatriates. There was often good reason for this reluctance. Commercial production might offer a lower net return than growing subsistence crops and foreign enterprises often offered low wages and poor working conditions. Yet from a European standpoint indigenous production or labour were essential both to provide private profit and to generate sufficient trade to support government and the cost of developing the infrastructure; and there was a consensus among all but a small minority of Europeans that in some way or other indigenous reluctance to work must be overcome.

It was, in fact, a special characteristic of colonialism, and one that has given it a bad reputation, that it facilitated the utilization of indigenous labour to develop a commercial economy and that colonial governments used or permitted methods of doing this that would not have been acceptable in European countries. One advantage of empire was that it facilitated the movement of labour across geographical boundaries. Migration took many forms. Until the mid-nineteenth century slave trading was the most common, along with voluntary migration of European settlers and the involuntary transportation of criminals. In the modern period, while slaving was banned and European migration continued, the most common method of bringing non-European labour from where it was in surplus to where it was needed was the labour contract by which a man committed himself, in return for his return passage and a defined level of wages, to work for a specified period (commonly one to three years) for the employer who paid for his transport; a system derived from indentures previously used to transport European workers to the Americas. Although political boundaries were not necessarily a bar to movements from one imperial system to another (for example, from Portuguese Mozambique to South Africa), on the whole each empire constituted a vast labour pool and the authorities encouraged mobility within its limits.

The results of these migrations are obvious from the demography of the modern world. Probably the largest single movement involving the longest distances was of Indians to Malaya, Burma, Ceylon, the Pacific, the Indian Ocean, East, Central and South Africa and the Caribbean. But examples can be found everywhere: Javanese to Sumatra; Chinese from Hong Kong to most parts of colonial Southeast Asia; Pacific islanders from one group to another and to Australia; and Africans within and between different groups of African colonies. To the post-colonial mind, preoccupied with the residual ethnic problems, the whole process may seem reprehensible. Yet at the time the real issue was whether this migration was voluntary and how well workers were treated: migration itself was accepted as a necessary part of a free trade world in which labour and capital had both to move freely.

There were, in fact, vast differences. At one extreme the Chinese normally moved on their own initiative and were genuine settlers. Indian 'coolies' were supposed to be volunteers, though it has been shown that many of them were tricked by professional recruiting agents on false pretences.[9] At the other extreme colonial governments in tropical Africa seem often to have assumed that every ablebodied man had an obligation to work for others if he was not already performing a socially or commercially useful function on his own behalf and that the state should, if necessary, ensure that he did so. This belief was deeply embedded in earlier European history and labour legislation (for example, the English vagrancy and poor laws) and it is not surprising that when Europeans penetrated Africa they were amazed to find that the 'work ethic' had little currency there. The common reaction was to believe that the 'moral regeneration' of the African peoples must begin with regular employment; and since this coincided with the economic interests of European employers and traders, it is easy to assume that it merely expressed self-interest. This is an over-simplification: belief in the moral function of regular work was common to most Christian missionaries from David Livingstone onwards.

Moreover, since metropolitan governments and private capitalists alike were initially very reluctant to invest in the new colonies, colonial authorities had to rely on their own resources to establish the foundations of modern societies; and of these labour was the only thing in relatively abundant supply. Hence one cannot blame the use of administrative pressure to compel Africans to work for others, whether locally or at a distance, simply on a cynical alliance between foreign capital and the colonial administration.

Unfortunately for the record of colonialism it often proved necessary to use methods unacceptable to humanitarians, then and later, to persuade Africans and some other indigenous peoples to undertake regular work or to produce for the market. This was partly because they were at first unaccustomed to the concept and unattracted by what they could buy with their wages. But, once this early phase was past, reluctance to take paid work was often due to the very low pay offered and the nature of the work. Neither poverty-stricken colonial governments nor, for example, owners of plantations producing for a highly competitive international market, could afford to pay wages comparable with those current in Europe. Thus in 1911 the Belgian government laid down a daily wage of 25 centimes (2.4d sterling) for full-time employees of the proposed Lever plantation enterprise in the Congo, Huileries du Congo Belge (HCB). To have paid more would have made HCB's palm oil uncompetitive with that produced under more favourable conditions in West Africa and South-east Asia; yet this low wage, coupled with the unpleasant nature of the work (climbing tall natural oil palms) which was traditionally slaves' work, made it almost impossible to recruit genuinely voluntary labour for this enterprise. Conversely it is significant that there was never a serious shortage of genuinely voluntary workers on the Rand gold mines which, despite deterrents such as danger and squalid living conditions, attracted workers from long distances by paying relatively high wages.

In these circumstances colonial governments found it necessary to use various forms of compulsion to get men out to work. As has been seen, it was an almost invariable practice to impose head or hut taxes to force people to take paid work. But this was seldom sufficient. Governments therefore resorted to physical compulsion. In the French and Portuguese African territories all men were liable to fixed periods of work without pay for the state and might be drafted to work for private employers if these were engaged on enterprises regarded as socially important. Almost everywhere European administrators put pressure on chiefs to provide labour for both public and private enterprises. Thus in the Belgian Congo it was normal as late as the early 1930s for government officials to tour rural areas with recruiting agents of the plantation companies and to order chiefs to provide a quota of 'voluntary' workers who were induced to sign indentures for periods of several years, which often involved travel over long distances and high wastage through disease.

These practices were undoubtedly characteristic of modern colonialism; but they must be seen in perspective. Forced labour has been found essential in the early states of modernization in all countries where labour is one of the few sources available for exploitation. Stalin used it in Russia and virtually every successor regime in the less-developed world has found it necessary to use various forms of compulsion. The main difference is that to the modern mind obligatory work is legitimate when demanded in the interests of a nation state but illegitimate when imposed by an alien colonial regime or to benefit private capital. It was the double misfortune of colonial regimes that they were responsible for the very first stages of modernization in most of the less-developed world but that they are not thought to have been morally qualified to use methods accepted as normal in totalitarian socialist societies.

Land utilization posed similar problems. The issue was as old as the first European settlements in America: had Europeans a moral right to occupy land used or claimed by indigenous peoples against their will? The traditional case for the settler and planter was that they would make more efficient use of land in the interests of humanity as a whole than the indigenous inhabitants, particularly if these were nomadic pastoralists. As William Lever, the British soap manufacturer, who was determined to establish tropical plantations in order to increase the supply of his raw materials, wrote in 1902, when he had been offered only a twenty-one year lease of land in Sierra Leone,

'I can never understand why a black man should be allowed ...
neither [to] develop his own land nor allow other people to do so'.[10]
Conversely humanitarian opinion from the later nineteenth century
increasingly claimed that non-Europeans had a moral right to the
land they actually used and should be properly compensated if they
chose to sell any part of it. Most of the debate that lasted throughout
the modern colonial period turned on these two issues: what constituted effective occupation of land by non-Europeans and what
could be regarded as reasonable compensation for evicting them.

On this count the main indictment of colonialism is that governments sometimes ignored the moral claims of indigenous peoples
and expropriated their land to satisfy the demands of white settlers
and other European enterprises. This was not universal.[11] In West
Africa, for example, both British and French governments from the
1890s adopted the principle that large European land ownership was
undesirable. As a result, by 1925 valid land concessions to Europeans
amounted to only 1 per cent of the area of the Gold Coast; and
in 1938 only 75,000 hectares of land in the Ivory Coast, the area
of French West Africa most intensively developed by foreign plantation companies, had been alienated in perpetuity. The situation
was very different elsewhere, particularly where there were many
white settlers. In South Africa by 1931 some six million Africans
occupied 'reserves' amounting to 34,000 square miles while 1.8 million Europeans occupied 440,000 square miles. In Southern
Rhodesia the Land Apportionment Act of 1930 gave Europeans,
who already owned 31 million acres, the right to buy 34 million acres
of Crown lands, while Africans, with reserves of 21 million acres,
were allotted a further seven million acres. In Northern Rhodesia
nearly 9 million acres had been alienated to Europeans by the 1930s.
Kenya provided the most controversial case. Large numbers of
Kikuyu had been moved off tribal territories to clear the White High-
lands for European farmers and in the 1930s the balance was 53,000
square miles of African reserves to 16,700 square miles of European
property and 99,000 square miles of Crown lands. In the French
Congo, where there was initially almost no commodity trade and
a thin population, the government granted vast concessions to forty
French companies in 1899 that covered 70 per cent of the territory,
though full ownership was conditional on improvements. This

extreme case demonstrated the weakness of making such vast concessions. By 1930, when all the original concessions lapsed, most of the companies had already been dissolved, very little development had occurred, and the few surviving enterprises were compensated for their efforts by being given, relatively, very small amounts of land.

This technique of granting large concessionary areas in the hope that European capitalists would select much smaller blocks and invest in communications and productive enterprises there was, nevertheless, adopted by the Portuguese in Mozambique and by the Belgians in the Belgian Congo after 1908. For example, William Lever's HCB was given the right to cull wild oil palm products within five circles, each of sixty kilometres radius.[12] The government's hope was that, since it lacked the resources to begin the development of the Congo, private enterprises of this kind would undertake the work in return for the right to exploit natural assets and ultimately to own the land they had improved. In the case of HCB these expectations were largely fulfilled: the company made a vast investment in communications and social services, established plantations in preferred areas, employed some 40,000 Africans by the 1950s and exported very large quantities of palm oil, palm kernels and other tropical products. In the end the company owned some 350,000 hectares of which it actively cultivated some 60,000. But this was exceptional. The majority of the early concessionary companies in all African, and also eastern, colonial territories achieved little, while disturbing the indigenous population and tying up vast areas which they could not or did not choose to develop. In the end it was left to the colonial governments to undertake the basic work of developing these territories at public expense.

It is, therefore, impossible to generalize usefully about the land policies adopted by the colonial powers. At one extreme they defended indigenous land ownership, at the other they might make vast concessions and pay only lip-service to the principle that indigenous rights must be protected. It is not even true that colonialism was solely responsible for large-scale European land ownership in the less-developed world since vast areas had been alienated by indigenous rulers in many places before formal European rule began, and the process would presumably have continued in any case. Yet there can be no doubt that colonialism greatly accelerated the process by giving greater security for foreign owners. In this way, and by ensuring a supply of labour for agricultural and mining enterprises, colonial rule assisted the evolution of a capitalist economy and commercial production and thus helped to integrate the colonies into the international economy. Some of the economic and social consequences of these developments will be examined in Part 3 of this chapter.

iii. Conclusion

There are, of course, many other aspects of colonialism which affected the economic and social life of the colonies – the character of the education system, the medical services, legal systems, and so on. But if one attempts to generalize about the characteristic and special consequences of colonialism one basic fact stands out. Every aspect of imperial policy was intended to 'open up' the dependencies to economic development by market forces, relying on the dynamics of the capitalist system in an 'open economy' to transform 'backward' into 'modern' societies. At the same time it was generally hoped to tie the colonial economies to that of each metropolis and thus, by social engineering, to wrench each from its geographical setting and integrate it into an imperial economy. These policies, in so far as they succeeded, constituted an irreversible change of direction for the colonial societies and the modern debate over colonialism largely turns on the outcome. To the left it appears that the colonies became mere 'satellites' of international capitalism, condemned to remain poor relations of the rich developed countries, providing them with the raw materials and markets they need but unable to restructure their own 'lop-sided' systems of production or to establish an industrial basis for sustained growth. To others it seems that colonialism was potentially a valuable device by which pre-capitalist societies could be helped to take the first steps along the well-worn path to affluence, even though the actual achievements of the colonial period were disappointingly small.

These conclusions are incompatible and it is the purpose of the following section to examine the impact of the 'open economy' on economic development of two main kinds – agriculture and industry

– in the colonies, using mainly evidence from three large colonial units belonging to different European states: India, French West Africa and the Belgian Congo. Two basic issues must be considered because they form part of a long-running controversy over the economic consequences of colonialism. First, whether the specialization in agricultural production for export that was characteristic of most colonial economies was good or bad for economic development. Second, whether the limited industrialization characteristic of most colonies was caused by colonialism and, conversely, what other factors may have been responsible.

3. Agriculture and industry in a colonial environment

i. Agriculture

One of the standard allegations against colonialism is that the colonial economy, moulded by metropolitan demand and local European interests, became excessively dependent on primary production of a limited range of commodities for export to the industrial countries. This, it has been argued, was bad for sound economic growth in two main ways. First, it resulted in 'lop-sided' economies in which the export sector grew disproportionately large while both subsistence agriculture for local consumption and also industrial production remained underdeveloped. Second, the commodity trade was itself undesirable in that the terms of trade between less- and more-developed countries deteriorated steadily over time, so that the colonial producer could obtain less with his labour than he could have done had he concentrated on producing food or other goods for himself or the local market. In other words, this was 'unequal exchange'. It is impossible to deny the general truth of the first proposition, though the reasons for limited industrialization will have to be considered later. First we must consider the case for and against specialization in production for the commodity export trade.

Concentration on primary commodity production was not peculiar to tropical colonies: it was an invariable feature of all economic systems in their formative years and it is therefore necessary to take account of countries which were not European dependencies or which, like Australia, were fully self-governing, in the period after 1870. Australia, for example, had one of the highest levels of *per capita* income in the world by the later nineteenth century, yet her economy was still based on the export of wool, gold, wheat, dairy products and minerals. The same was true, though with a different mix of products, of Canada, New Zealand and South Africa and had until recently been the case with the USA. The underlying question must therefore be why these 'new' societies had been able to base their sustained economic growth on specialized primary production of this type while the modern colonies did not, at least before 1945.

A first consideration must be the type of production employed in different places. For analytical purposes modes of production may crudely be divided into capitalist enterprises and pre-capitalist (or 'peasant') production within a traditional economic and social framework. The following list gives some indication of the main patterns, though it is not exclusive.

Types of agricultural production outside Europe

I. CAPITALIST

i. Individual European-style farms

Australia, Canada, New Zealand, South Africa, the USA, etc.; and also in parts of the Belgian Congo, Kenya, French and Italian North Africa: food grains, meat, wool, dairy products.

ii. Plantations, normally owned by companies and employing consider-able amounts of non-European labour

Australia: sugar in Queensland.

Belgian Congo: oil palms, coffee, rubber, cocoa, tea, etc.

India: tea, coffee.

Ceylon: tea, coffee, coconuts.

Malaya: rubber and oil palms.

Indonesia: rubber, sugar, tobacco, coffee, coconuts.

French West Africa: coffee, cocoa, bananas, etc., mainly in Ivory Coast. (Also in East Africa, parts of central and East Africa, Indo-China, the Caribbean and the Pacific.)

iii. Forestry

Large-scale forestry companies in most colonial areas.

II. NON-CAPITALIST

i. *Commercial export commodities*

West Africa: oil palm products, cocoa, cotton, ground-nuts, coffee, bananas, shea-nuts, etc.

Malaya: rubber, palm oil, tin.

India: cotton, indigo, wheat, jute, sugar, rice.

Indonesia: sugar, rubber, tobacco, copra.

Belgian Congo: cotton, oil palms, coffee, rubber.

East Africa: cotton, coffee.

ii. *Subsistence*

Virtually all food for local consumption was grown by the indigenous people within the traditional sector of the economy and normally by unimproved methods; though in some places there was a substantial import of food grains.

This rough summary draws attention to some important features of production in the colonies. First, although plantations have conventionally been taken as the normal method of production, they were not in fact as important overall as non-capitalistic production. Plantations were used because a crop was new to a particular place and required capital and skills beyond those available locally. Alternatively they might be necessary because insufficient local labour was available and immigrant labour could only be used within a capitalist environment. Conversely there was little or no incentive to establish plantations where indigenous production of an export commodity was already established or where it was readily adopted by indigenous land owners: the classic example of the latter is cocoa in the Gold Coast and Nigeria. Indeed, almost all the main export crops of West Africa were at all times peasant products. Moreover, even though a new product might be introduced on plantations, it was often taken up by local peasants, as happened in Indonesia and elsewhere.

It is an open question whether plantations owned and run by foreigners were an asset to a developing colonial economy. On the credit side they were historically the best means of introducing new crops, attracting foreign capital and skills, expanding the cash economy and the wage-labour force, providing foreign exchange and increasing agricultural productivity. As against this, foreign investment involved repatriation of profits. Plantations tended to be owned and run by expatriates, possibly excluding local producers from profitable fields of activity; though in India at least many plantations had been acquired by Indians long before independence. They required labour, which was often poorly paid and semi-servile; and immigration caused social problems. Because of their relatively large capital and inflexibility they tended to commit a developing economy to certain products, even if these ceased to be profitable in relation to changing market conditions. Finally, they tended to constitute an alien enclave which might provide few benefits for the local economy in terms of reinvested profits or transferred skills.

But on balance plantations can best be seen as valuable to those territories which possessed a comparative advantage in factor endowment (particularly the right climatic conditions) and where there was an ample local labour supply because they increased employment, stimulated the cash economy, raised levels of productivity and earned foreign exchange which could be used to finance development. They could, moreover, be bought out or expropriated and run by indigenous entrepreneurs or successor governments. It is significant that in the 1970s many new states still depended heavily on the export earnings of plantations and that some countries were inviting foreign companies to establish new plantations in co-operation with the state. In short, the special advantage of the plantation in a less-developed colonial economy was that it meant the injection of relatively efficient capitalist methods into an economy with generally low levels of agricultural productivity.

Peasant production of commercial export crops also had its benefits and drawbacks. On the credit side it implied no destruction of the social order, did not deprive the indigenous peoples of their land and left them as independent producers with the possibility of developing into prosperous farmers. Peasant production was relatively price elastic, and better fitted to alter its patterns of production to meet market changes than plantations. A peasant sugar producer in India, for example, could grow a different crop one year if the price of sugar fell, whereas a West Indian sugar plantation owner could only produce and sell sugar on a falling market. At its best, as in cocoa production in the Gold Coast, peasant agriculture could be very efficient and generate a prosperous community of specialized farmers. On the debit side, however, peasant production was more likely to mean low productivity due to perpetuation of primitive techniques, often within communal agricultural systems. It could not readily absorb large amounts of capital because the scale of operation remained small and the traditional response to demand was to increase the area under cultivation rather than improve methods. Thus, while peasant production of export crops might initially raise the standard of living of the producers in that they were exploiting resources of land, labour and savings which might otherwise have remained idle (the 'vent for surplus', as it has been called) it also tended to be unprogressive beyond a certain point. To contribute successfully to economic growth the peasant farmer had, like the wheat growers of the Punjab or the cocoa growers of West Africa, to come to resemble the European farmer rather than the tradition-bound peasant of many parts of Africa and Asia.

Indeed, the basic defect of both the plantation and peasant modes of export production was that they evaded the real economic and social problem of tropical agriculture – how to achieve increased output and higher quality without alienating the means of production to expatriates. There were two alternative means of doing this, one capitalistic, the other socialist. The first implied progressive individualization of land tenures, cheap credit, adequate technical advice, irrigation, etc., all of which proved successful in the relatively few places in which they were applied, for example in the Punjab and the Gezira cotton scheme in the Egyptian Sudan. In most places, however, governments were frightened of the social and political resistance a policy of individualizing tenures aroused and were unable or unwilling to provide the other facilities needed. This double failure, of aim and method, represents one of the great failures of modern colonialism. Despite the devoted efforts of agricultural specialists working with very limited resources, colonial agriculture remained in the 1940s relatively inefficient in most countries. Conversely, although some attempts were made in the later years of the colonial period, particularly after 1945, to stimulate collective agriculture of a modern type through co-operatives of various kinds, it was inconsistent with the character of the imperial countries to impose true collective agriculture on the pattern developed by social-ist states. Whether such a policy could be successful is still open to question, though post-colonial governments are experimenting with it in several African and Asian countries. It is at least certain that the colonial state lacked the authority to undertake such vast schemes of social engineering successfully.

The second main question connected with primary production for export is its relative advantage from the standpoint of the colonial society as an alternative to production of foodstuffs and other goods for local consumption: ground-nuts instead of rice in the western Sudan, and so on. The evidence of a number of colonies suggests that the comparative advantage arising from these alternatives varied widely according to three main variables: the relative return to producers in different places, determined by climate, soil, trans-port costs, marketing arrangements, etc.; whether 'underutilized' labour and land were available for growing export crops without reducing food supplies; and whether local consumption exceeded the supply of food crops. The case of India shows the economic benefit of specialization in export crops. Although in the early nine-teenth century indigo was mostly grown under economic compulsion and was generally unprofitable for producers, jute and sugar were both grown voluntarily for the local and export market as an addi-tion to subsistence production and the area used for these closely reflected market prices. Wheat and rice were grown for export as well as for local consumption so long as there was a surplus and then largely ceased to be an export crop. Cotton was a marginal crop grown voluntarily by peasants as a source of income and production was extremely price elastic. These crops made a significant contribu-tion to Indian economic development. They gave flexibility to peasant agriculture, expanded the cash economy, provided export earnings and in the case of jute, cotton and sugar, provided raw materials for nascent Indian industries. Most important, these were the dynamic elements in Indian agriculture, constrasting sharply with the virtually static condition of most non-exported food grains. By the 1960s it was this type of crop that at last generated progressive mechanized agriculture in many parts of the sub-continent.[13]

Indeed, the real weakness of agricultural production in India was in food for local consumption. Neither methods of production nor the quality of the product improved significantly and units of production tended to become smaller as population pressed on available land. Since there was almost no mechanization or use of improved seeds, output of food grains expanded less than population, at an annual average rate of 0.11 per cent in the period 1891–1941, as compared with an increase of 0.67 per cent for cash crops. Conversely, while productivity per acre devoted to food grains fell by an average of 0.18 per cent, productivity of non-food grain crops increased by an average of 0.86 per cent annually.[14] Comparable figures are not available for other colonies; but it seems very unlikely that productivity in the traditional sector of most colonial economies increased significantly, even though the acreage devoted to it expanded to meet demand. Such figures, if they are at all reliable, suggest that, in India at least, despite the many defects in the system of commodity production, specialization in cash export crops may well have had significant advantages over subsistence production as a means of sustaining or improving real incomes. There availability of food grains was improved in the face of declining *per capita* Indian production by imports of food grains, which in turn were paid for by exports of commodity crops. This constituted an example of the operation of the principle of comparative advantage.

The difficulty is to decide whether this was generally true of other colonial territories for which comparable statistics are not available. In British and French West Africa, for example, which were geared to the commodity export trade and where most agriculture was in the hands of peasants, conditions were very different. There were, perhaps, three main potential obstacles to full realization in these colonies of the benefits of specialized production for export: adverse trends in the terms of trade; imperfect competition both in the commodity market and in consumer goods; and the relatively high cost of transport, particularly to producers far from the coastal ports. Collectively, it has been argued, these adverse factors offset the advantages to be expected from specialization in commodity production to the point at which less favoured producers in bad times actually lost their involvement in the market economy and would have been better off had they continued to grow subsistence crops for their own consumption. These allegations can be investigated in relation to French West Africa on which a considerable amount of work has been done.

First, as to the terms of trade. Suret-Canale has argued that 'the development ... was generally unfavourable, with marked depressions in periods of crisis and war followed by recoveries that rarely, except for very short periods, reestablished the earlier buying power'. To support this he showed that between 1913 and 1930 the coefficient of the price increase for ground-nuts was 3.4 and for cotton fabric, a main African purchase, 7.6; while between 1913 and 1931 the amount of rice purchased by 100 kilos of ground-nuts dropped from 110 to 42.8 kilos.[15] But other estimates give different results. J.-J. Poquin has shown that the terms of trade of the main export commodities of French West Africa fluctuated very widely between 1925 and 1938 and that the capacity to import, which takes account of increased volume of export production, almost doubled in this period. There was a large variation between different products, but overall the terms of trade were no worse in 1938 than they had been in 1925. The Second World War resulted in a serious deterioration in both terms of trade and capacity to import, but by 1955 the index of the former (1938 = 100) had risen to 215 and of the latter to 244.[16] These figures suggest that, while an export-oriented economy was very vulnerable to international conditions, there was no overall or long-term deterioration in the terms of trade of French West Africa. More detailed investigation also shows that different products fared very differently, and this helps to explain why some parts of the federation fared so much better than others.

The second main factor influencing the profitability of export production in West Africa was the oligopolistic system of marketing through large foreign trading houses. There is no doubt that in French West Africa, as throughout the region, competition for buying cash crops was imperfect. There were three major trading firms, two French and the Anglo-Dutch firm Unilever, which operated through French subsidiaries. In 1938 the three Unilever subsidiaries alone exported from French West Africa, Togo, Cameroun, and French Equatorial Africa 25 per cent of ground-nuts in shell, 16 per cent of decorticated ground-nuts, 23.7 per cent of palm oil, 32 per cent of palm kernels, 57 per cent of shea-butter, 35 per cent of shea-nuts, 23.8 per cent of cocoa and 15 per cent of coffee.[17]

These big firms also dominated the import trade. In 1949 the three largest between them imported 73 per cent of the sugar, 66 per cent of the rice and 45 per cent of the flour sold in Senegal.[18] It is more difficult to determine whether these firms exploited their position to extract unreasonably large profits, since insufficient research has yet been done; but Suret-Canale and others have alleged that these companies were able to depress the price actually paid to producers well below levels that were justified by the current state of the international market.[19] To the extent that this was the case it obviously reduced the advantage the peasant received from specialization in cash crops; though it must be said that the system of state marketing adopted by British territories in West Africa during the Second World War and by the French territories later may well have had a more adverse effect on the return to the African farmer.

It seems likely in any case that other factors, notably climate, soil and the cost of transporting export products to the coast, had as large, if not a larger, effect on the reward the farmer received in different parts of French West Africa. The table on p. 87, showing the composition of export prices for 1953 (admittedly seven years after this survey ends), is based on a survey undertaken by the federal government of French West Africa and gives an indication of the relative importance of various factors affecting the return to the farmer. Commodities are divided into two categories, according to whether they were high or low price products; and areas of production near the coast are italicized to contrast these with areas inland from which transport costs were relatively high.

These statistics, if they are relevant to the colonial period as a whole, suggest some important conclusions about the profitability of export commodities to the producer and to the French West African economy. First, the profit margins were relatively small. Second, the most variable factor was transport which, due partly to the relative inefficiency of the region's internal transport system and to the immense distance of the interior producing regions from the coast, made a critical difference to the proportion of the export price of goods received by the producer: only 42 per cent for the man growing ground-nuts inland at Maradi but 64 per cent at Kaolack, on the coast of Senegal; 37 per cent for gum at Timbuktu as against 58 per cent at Ferlo. These figures suggest the conclusion

Composition of export price of French West African export commodities (percentage of price free on board)

product	place	producer	taxes	transport	processing	wastage	company profit
i. High value commodities							
ground-nuts	*Kaolack*	64	15.5	3.2	6.3	0.4	10.6
	Maradi	42	11.1	28	7	1.1	10.8
coffee	*Bouaké*	71.4	17.1	1.7	2	1.6	6.2
cocoa	*Dimbokro*	64.7	21	1.8	3.5	1.6	7.3
cotton	*Bouaké*	65.2	6.6	2.4	15.5	0.3	10
	Koutrala	62.2	6.6	13.2	10	0.3	7.7
kapok	Kayes	42	11.7	10	25	0.8	10.5
ii. Low value commodities							
palm kernels	*Zinguinchor*	70	12	—	11.4	1.4	5.2
palm oil	*Bohicon*	65.7	10	3	8	1.7	11.6
gum arabic	*Ferlo*	58	10	7.9	13.7	4.9	5.5
	Timbuktu	37	9.3	29	8.3	4.8	11.6
shea-nuts	*Kandi*	44	3.9	24.8	17.3	2.8	7.2
	Bamako	30.8	0.8	29	21	8	10.4
rice	Niger	52.4	—	20	15	1.6	11

Source: J.-J. Poquin, *Les relations économiques extérieurs des pays d'Afrique noire de l'union française* (Paris 1957), pp. 102–4.

that, while most products were desirable from the standpoint of the country as a whole, in that they resulted in export earnings, and from that of the merchant, since he obtained a profit, some were not rewarding to the producer in less favoured regions. The real criticism that can be levelled against colonial governments is thus that they put pressure on Africans to grow crops for export in some regions where it was uneconomic to do so as an alternative to growing food for their own subsistence.

These variations within a single political region of part of sub-Saharan Africa suggest that it would be wrong to reach any general conclusion as to whether it was in the best interests of colonial peasant producers and of the colonial economy as a whole to concentrate on commodity production for export, for similar contrasts could be shown between different crops in each part of the many colonial territories of Africa and the East. On the one hand the use of indigenous resources for this purpose undoubtedly benefited some producers in most colonies and most colonial economies overall. On the other hand the imperial authorities seem to have been too keen to stimulate commodity production to meet the needs of the metropolitan economies, to generate trade on which taxes could be levied to sustain the colonial governments, even to please trading enterprises; with the result that they sometimes built up patterns of production that could not be justified in terms of comparative advantage. The result was what Marxists describe as 'uneven development': in West Africa comparatively high incomes in the favoured regions such as the Gold Coast, Ivory Coast, Senegal and parts of Nigeria, comparative poverty in areas such as Mali and Niger to which an export-oriented economy was unsuited. But whether any other pattern of economic development, even under a post-colonial independent regime, could have solved the economic problems of these intrinsically poor regions remains an open question.

ii. Industrialization and diversification under colonialism

a. Obstacles to industrialization in the colonies

The absence of industrialization and of diversification from the relatively narrow economic base provided by concentration on export commodities are the other features commonly alleged to have been characteristic of colonial economies. The accusation may take a positive or negative form: either the colonial powers refused to permit industrialization or they merely failed to promote it. We must examine the evidence for and against these hypotheses, concentrating mainly on the record of India, French West Africa and the Belgian Congo.

It is undeniable that the colonial powers did not positively encourage industrialization in any of their dependencies before 1945 (though thereafter most of them took active steps to promote it) and that in some ways their basic economic policies discouraged it. The main reasons are clear. As has been seen above, economic theories in vogue before the later 1930s were adverse to 'artificial' devices calculated to promote industrialization. Free traders believed in specialization in the interests of maximum efficiency and saw no benefits to a colony in establishing import-substituting industries which could not survive without heavy protection. Neo-mercantilists assumed that colonies should provide markets for metropolitan manufacturers. Humanitarians suspected urbanization as a threat to indigenous society. It is, therefore, not surprising that imperial governments were happy to see the colonies remaining primary producers.

On the other hand no imperial government actually went so far as to ban manufactures in the colonies in the modern period; and it is therefore necessary to consider why these did not develop autonomously as they had done in Europe, North America and Japan. One likely source of investment in industry was the industrialist or financier in the developed countries, since these were eventually responsible for much of the industrial investment that took place after 1945. A.K. Sen has argued that in the Indian case there was a consensus among British industrialists, who might have been expected to invest in production there, that they should not do so in order to preserve British primacy.[20] This is difficult to prove or disprove; but there were in fact much stronger economic reasons why European industrialists and capitalists should have been reluctant to establish subsidiaries or new enterprises in the less-developed colonies before the First World War, and in many places until the 1950s.

Manufacturing firms with an established export market would set up subsidiaries only if it seemed more profitable to manufacture locally, for the local or the international market, than at home. Then, and in the later twentieth century, their assessment of possibilities in any one place was conditioned by three main variables: the relative cheapness of factors of production at home or overseas; the size of the local market, which decided whether there would be economies of scale; and the degree of effective protection, whether provided by tariffs, physical controls or factors such as the cost of importing raw materials or manufactures. During the century before 1945 the balance of advantage on all three counts was tilted against local production in almost all less-developed countries, whether colonies or independent states. Factors of production might be cheap in the colonies (low wages, local raw materials) but these were generally more than offset by other considerations. An untrained labour force was inefficient and it was necessary at first to employ a disproportionate number of European supervisors at salaries much above those paid in Europe. Few colonies produced all the raw materials needed for a particular product and the cheapness of those available might be offset by the high cost of importing others and also intermediates, such as packing materials. In addition, limitations of the infrastructure – inadequate power and water supplies, dear transport, poor health and educational facilities – coupled with undeveloped marketing facilities, were deterrents. Further, the market for consumer goods was usually very restricted, except in large countries such as India or Indonesia. Finally, given free trade or free import from a metropolis, effective protection depended on natural factors. Although these might be significant, as in the Congo, they were seldom sufficient to offset the other diseconomies of producing in a less-developed country for a limited market.

These considerations did not, of course, necessarily apply with the same force to non-Europeans in the colonies or to European settlers there. For these there was not the alternative of exporting to the colony from the metropolis: the colony provided their only opportunity. If they operated on a small scale they could avoid the high overheads of a foreign company and might prosper by exploiting a small regional market, thus evading the problem of national distribution. Being local, they might also have a better 'feel' for the local

market. Such men did, indeed, perform an important role in the early
industrialization of many colonies; yet there were many common
obstacles: lack of indigenous entrepreneurial talent; shortage of
long-term capital; limitation of local markets; and the effects of the
'open door' to overseas goods.

Of these the last two have already been considered: they affected
local as much as foreign would-be industrialists, though not necessarily to the same extent. Although individuals with the requisite
ability could be found almost everywhere, the comparative lack of
entrepreneurial talent was common to nearly all the colonies.[21] The
problem was that what talent there was was seldom geared to
mechanized industrial production which, in its European form, was
so alien to most colonial societies that even in India, in many ways
a very advanced economy, it took about a century of contact with
the British before special groups, led by the Parsis, were prepared
to invest in factories on their own initiative. After very much shorter
periods of intensive contact with western technology, and starting
from a less advanced base, it is not surprising that very few other
colonial territories had reached the same point by 1945. It must also
be said that before the 1940s few locally based European enterprises
offered non-Europeans the opportunity to gain experience of mana-
gerial and technical skills. Finally, even those non-Europeans who
became 'achievement oriented' and wished to establish local industries found it very difficult to raise the necessary capital. In many
parts of Asia there was ample latent capital available in land, gold,
jewels and the profits of trade; the difficulty was to harness it for
investment in industry, given established preferences and the absence
of a stock market. In most other parts of the colonial world capital
itself was in very short supply and entrepreneurs would have to depend heavily on credit. Here there were difficulties. As has been seen,
most European banks concentrated on exchange activities connected
with overseas trade and on short-term rather than medium- or long-
term credit. British banking law in fact imposed strict limits on
provision of credit. But even if credit was available, the would-be
indigenous industrialist commonly found that his credit was poor
because he could provide no firm security: here communal land
ownership was a serious obstacle. A few non-Europeans, notably
the Levantines in West Africa, Indians in East and Central Africa

and the Chinese in South-east Asia, surmounted these difficulties by using private funds and reinvesting most of their profits. But for most colonial subjects lack of credit was an insurmountable bar to industrial investment.

b. Industrialization in India, French West Africa and the Belgian Congo

With so many different factors involved the course and extent of industrialization inevitably differed in every European dependency. It is therefore proposed to outline very briefly the main trends in two territories – India and French West Africa – which between them represent the greatest and one of the least achievements by 1945, and in the Belgian Congo, where the level of industrialization lay between these two. Emphasis will in each case be placed on factors determining the extent of industrial investment and the relative importance of foreign and indigenous capital and enterprise.

India

The century after 1850 divides into two unequal periods. Until about 1920 industrial development was limited to a relatively few products and expatriates played a leading role. In the next thirty years the industrial base broadened considerably, industry ceased to be a small enclave in a traditional agricultural economy and became its main growing point and Indians played an increasingly important role.

Until the 1920s industrial development was restricted almost entirely to cotton, jute and iron. The cotton industry was the first and most important. India produced raw cotton for export and had a long tradition of hand manufacture.[22] Adoption of alien technology was therefore natural and easy, helped immensely by the contemporary development of railways and coal-mining to provide distribution and power. As in Britain, spinning came first to serve hand weaving. The first mill was built in Bombay in 1854 and by 1914 India had 271 mills with 6.8 million spindles and 104,000 looms. This industry arose spontaneously from the conjuncture of traditional Indian commerce and western technology under conditions of free trade. Most early mills were established by Parsi merchants who had long exported cotton yarn and cloth and who now saw the need to use European machines to spin yarn so that their cloth could compete with exports from Manchester. For long management was in the hands of Europeans employed by the mill-owners: as late as 1925 the proportion was still 28.4 per cent, though few were left by 1945. But ownership was always predominantly Indian, and in 1931 it was estimated that 99 per cent of the capital was in Indian hands. Most important, cotton textiles showed that where conditions were favourable, with local raw materials, ample labour that quickly adapted to factory conditions, and a large market at home and abroad for cotton yarn and cloth of a relatively coarse type which was therefore not competing directly with British and other imports, it was perfectly possible for a colonial dependency to establish large-scale modern industry under free trade conditions. The protective duties imposed in the 1920s increased profit margins but were not essential to the existence of the industry.

The only other factory industry of any importance in India during the nineteenth century was jute.[23] It had much in common with cotton in that it began in the 1850s with the import of British yarn-spinning equipment to produce cheaper and better yarn for the indigenous weavers of 'gunny bags', but power looms were soon added. The industry was from the first concentrated in Calcutta for proximity to the areas in which jute was grown and it was made possible by the building of railways to the Raniganj coal field. From the 1870s a large export trade developed in competition with Dundee and by 1932 there were 60,000 looms employing 263,000 workers. In all these respects jute closely resembled cotton. The main difference was that the industry was started by Europeans resident in India. Although by the 1930s half, and by 1950 three-quarters, of the capital was owned by Indians, the management remained largely European.[24] This made jute perhaps the most typically 'colonial' of early Indian industries.

Apart from coal-mining, which expanded rapidly from the 1850s and played a critical role in the modernization of the Indian economy, iron and steel was the last major industry established in India before 1914; and its origins are of particular importance in that they demonstrate many of the factors making for and against industrialization in a colonial situation. The basic question, given the presence of ample coal and iron ore deposits in close proximity in Bengal and the Central Provinces, has for long been why these were not exploited on a large scale before the establishment of the Tata business in 1907. It was certainly not, as some Indian nationalists and others have argued, because the government discouraged it: the provincial governments helped several small enterprises considerably, and the Viceroy, Lord Curzon, encouraged Tata in 1906–1907. There were technical difficulties connected with the quality of Indian coking coal; but the main obstacle lay in a limited market coupled with strong overseas competition. The size of the market can be gauged from the import of iron and steel goods: 262,000 tons in 1900 and an average of 808,000 tons between 1909 and 1914. Without tariff protection it was extremely difficult for any new Indian enterprise to compete with German, British and American iron or steel products and the fact that there was very little secondary industry consuming ferrous metals made the situation very unpromising. J.N. Tata, the Parsi cotton magnate, seems, therefore, to have been motivated by nationalist as much as by economic considerations in his attempts to start an indigenous iron and steel industry in the 1880s which came to fruition in 1907. His enterprise succeeded mainly because the First World War provided unlimited demand and then, when disaster threatened in 1922–3 during the post-war slump, because the government could at last provide tariff protection. By 1931 the level of protection was between 15 and 21 per cent and the government gave priority to Tata's and three other Indian companies in providing such critical products as steel rails and rolling-stock for the railways. In 1939 total Indian production was 842,900 tons and imports were down to 257,000 tons. By 1945 production was about 1,150,000 tons and thereafter the Indian producers virtually monopolized the market. Between 1946 and 1951 average net profits in the industry as a whole were 11.7 per cent of net asset value.[25]

Although the Indian iron and steel industry was started before 1914, its success was certain only after 1923; and it therefore belongs to the second phase of industrialization that began in the 1920s and was made possible by a combination of tariff protection and a growing market for consumer goods. The results cannot be described in detail, but by 1945 two striking changes had occurred. First, India was by then self-sufficient in a wide range of consumer goods: by 1943 some 60 per cent of the market was held by Indian firms.

Second, although foreign capital had pioneered a number of new industries, such as soap, vegetable ghee, rubber tyres and electronics, many others had been started by Indians and Indians owned most of the capital in the earlier industries. In banking Indians handled some 83 per cent of deposits by 1947 and Indian firms handled around 60 per cent of the import/export trade by 1952. These developments can be seen in contrasting ways. The nationalist can emphasize that the capital goods industry was still very small and that the share of modern industry in total national income was low. The entrepreneurial base was narrow and virtually all technology was imported.[26] On the other hand such criticisms overlook the basic difficulty of transforming an agricultural economy of the Indian type: post-independence governments have made very little impact on the problem. It is true that the British authorities in India did little before the 1920s to stimulate industrial development, yet in the last two decades of the colonial period there they adopted a deliberate 'national' policy by means of tariffs, quotas and, during the war, very strict control of the economy as a whole. Indeed, the 'managed' economy of post-independence India was largely planned and partly executed by the British under the stimulus of the war. All this suggests that while colonialism had not encouraged industrialization it was not a bar to it and that once the British accepted the need for the state to help industry at home they were prepared to follow the same course in any dependency which possessed the capacity to respond. Industrial growth, particularly in the basic industries and technology, was much faster after 1947 than before, helped by an unprecedented degree of public and foreign investment. But it is unhistorical to compare developments in the modern era of state initiative, which was common to Europe as well as India and other less-developed countries, with what happened under the conditions of an 'open economy' before 1945. By that standard the achievement of India was substantial.

The Belgian Congo

In terms of industrial development the Congo lies somewhere between the big Asian dependencies, such as India and Indonesia, with their very large populations that provided a stimulating market for industrial investment, and, on the other extreme, the majority of small and poor countries in Africa, the Caribbean and the Pacific, which had small populations and in which industrialization was very limited both under colonialism and afterwards. By contrast with this last group the Congo had four major aids to industrialization. By African standards it had a large population – some ten million in 1947 – which included about 34,000 Europeans, mostly engaged in administration or mining, who were comparatively affluent. Second, the mining industry – copper, diamonds, gold, manganese, etc. – generated comparatively large urban communities and relatively large African incomes, which provided a reasonable market for consumer goods. Third, there were reasonably good supplies of power and adequate communications by rail and river to distribute industrial products. Finally, although the Congo remained free-trading until after 1945 and the government gave industry no direct help, the combination of revenue-producing import duties, the high cost of freight on imported goods and the availability of a wide range of local raw materials combined to give some effective protection to local industry.

The result of these and other favourable factors was that the Congo was unique among African countries, excluding South Africa and Southern Rhodesia, in the growth and relative importance of its consumer industries. In 1958, two years before independence, the Congo had an African wage-earning labour force of 1,102,000, 8.2 per cent of the population. Of this labour force 10.6 per cent were employed in manufacturing industry in 1959. As a proportion of the total production of goods, industrial products constituted an average of 30.2 per cent between 1950 and 1958, of which 10.6 per cent was processing of agricultural products, 13.4 per cent manufacture for the local market and 6.2 per cent construction materials.[27] In the 1950s the average share of industry in the gross domestic product of the Congo, 25 per cent, put her in the second United Nations category of underdeveloped countries, even though actual average incomes were within the lowest category. The question to be answered is how and why this industrial development took place within a basically poor and agricultural country and what light it sheds on the character of colonialism.

It would be convenient to divide industry into those branches concerned with processing primary products for export and those serving the domestic market and substituting for imports; but this distinction is not always clear. The processing of some primary products, such as cotton, vegetable oil and coffee served both purposes, as did a wide range of building materials and timber. On the other hand chemical products, textiles and a wide range of consumer goods were made almost entirely for local consumption. The two categories of industry in fact developed simultaneously in conformity with the cyclical trends in the economy. The first phase took place in the 1920s, when cement, soap, sugar, cotton textiles, beer and other industries were set up for the first time: between 1925 and 1929 industrial production grew at more than 12 per cent a year.[28] But with the dramatic slump in exports, and therefore incomes, in the early 1930s manufacturing also declined, and by 1935 the index of domestic industrial production was back to the level of 1920. Recovery began in 1935 and from then until 1949 industrial production expanded at an annual growth rate of 14 per cent, regaining the 1929 level in 1944. In the following decade considerable new investment took place, helped by booming exports, the great influx of new capital and the Ten Year Plan. From 1950 to 1957 industrial production grew at an average rate of 14.3 per cent, but declined in 1957–9 with the falling off of exports and fears of decolonization.[29] Thus, although industrial development over the whole period after 1920 grew much faster than the production of export commodities, industrialization was essentially a by-product of the general performance of the economy and followed the same cyclical trends. This in turn implies that industry was merely an adjunct of an economy that was still based on agriculture and mining.

Yet the rate of growth and the increase in productivity in the industrial sector, especially after 1945, were impressive and generally higher than those in mining and agriculture. Between 1933, the lowest point for industry after 1920, and 1939 the total value of industrial production increased from 203.5 to 422.7 million francs at constant 1950 prices. If the value added to palm oil products by processing, which constituted more than half the industrial product in 1933, is excluded, production increased from 79.9 to 224.6 million francs in the same years. Between 1949 and 1958 the index of industrial production (1947–9 = 100) rose from 118 to 350.[30] From 1950 to 1958 the index of productivity in industry rose from 100 to 258.2, as compared with an increase from 100 to 211.4 in mining and to 186.9 in European-owned agriculture.[31] These were impressive results by any standard.

Apart from its close dependence on a demand that fluctuated with the performance of the Congo's commodity exports (mining and agricultural products) industry in the Congo had two special features that may be regarded as typical of an underdeveloped colonial economy. First, a very large proportion of all major industrial activities were in, or relatively close to, the two main towns, Elizabethville and Leopoldville, the main exceptions being processing plants near the source of their raw materials. Thus in 1957 53.7 per cent of the total product of manufacturing and food processing took place in the Bas-Congo and Leopoldville zone and 26.8 per cent of all construction, though this area produced only 19.1 per cent of the gross domestic product of the colony.[32] These concentrations were the product of different factors. In Katanga the attractive force was the copper industry, the large wage-earning population and the industry's ancillary needs. In Leopoldville the fact that it was above the rapids on the Congo, which cut Boma and Matadi off from the interior, provided an incentive to establish industries which could serve the vast areas up river. Once each of these centres was established with adequate power and other services, it was natural that new industries should be attracted there. Hence the disproportionate growth of modern industries in these places which, it has been argued, also acted as 'poles of development', stimulating a wide range of economic activities in the regions they served.[33]

The other special feature of industry in the Congo, which distinguished it from the Indian case and perhaps constituted its most typically colonial characteristic, was that a large proportion of these enterprises were subsidiaries of the very large foreign-owned companies that dominated all aspects of the Congolese economy. This was not true of all sectors of industry. There was a very large number of small firms, especially in construction, where the number of firms increased from 248 in 1950 to 600 in 1957[34], and also in the service industries. But it was natural that in enterprises requiring substantial amounts of capital the large European corporations that had operated there from the first decades of the century should use their local knowledge and profits to diversify their activities as the market broadened.[35] Thus the Société Générale subsidiary, Compagnie du Congo pour le Commerce et l'Industrie (CCCI) set up in 1920 one of the first cement companies, Société des Ciments du Congo, which produced 300,000 tons of cement in 1960. In 1920, also, CCCI established Compagnie Cotonnière Congolaise which dominated the cotton ginning industry and in turn set up a group of subsidiary textile companies at Leopoldville which manufactured cotton cloth, blankets and sacking. The other big investment companies followed similar policies on a rather smaller scale, notably the Groupe Empain, Groupe de la Comminière, Groupe Lambert and Unilever, which, in addition to its main plantation company, Huileries du Congo Belge, had a large trading business and a soap and margarine factory at Leopoldville.

This concentration of ownership of the expanding industrial sector in the hands of a few Belgian and British firms, which existed also in other parts of Africa where the local economy pivotted round one or more large extractive or plantation ventures (such as Northern Rhodesia), or where, as in West Africa the import/export trade was controlled by similar foreign companies, clearly distinguished industrialization in the Congo from that in India, Indonesia and other Asian countries, and also from that in African colonies such as Southern Rhodesia and Kenya, where local European settlers and Indians played a far more important role. For the Congo this trend had both good and bad effects. Its advantage was that these big firms, which possessed very large resources of money and skills, could react very quickly to a perceived economic opportunity, establishing relatively large and efficient factories, etc., to meet demand. The Congo therefore avoided the constraint imposed on many poor countries by lack of industrial capital. On the other hand these large concerns seldom used Africans in senior posts: indeed there was something near to a job reservation convention until the later 1950s. Africans therefore had little opportunity to learn how to run a modern industry and the presence of these big factories, whose production was tailored to the size of the market, acted as a disincentive to others, whether African or foreign, to start competing ventures. In this sense the industrial sector of the Congo was in foreign hands and after independence in 1960 it proved a slow and difficult process for

Africans to take the initiative in expanding the industrial base of the economy.

French West Africa

The history of industrialization in the nine colonies of the federation of French West Africa represents a third model, more characteristic of much of the less-developed world than either India or the Congo. At first sight the federation might seem to offer favourable conditions for industrial growth. With a total population of twenty-six million in 1960 it was one of the largest free trade areas in Africa, much larger than the Congo. Although defenceless against imports from France, local industrialists had ample tariff protection against imports from other places. The large export of commodities such as ground-nuts, coffee, cocoa, etc. made it likely that processing of these crops would stimulate industrial activities. Yet French West Africa lacked some of the key advantages the Congo possessed. There were, comparatively, very few affluent Europeans to provide a market for the more expensive consumer goods. Mining enterprises were smaller and more dispersed. Above all the federation was not protected by distance and the cost of freight, as was the Congo. Freight charges from Europe to West Africa on most goods were so low that they might not balance the higher overheads to be expected in a small local factory as compared with those in a large enterprise in France. To these adverse factors must be added lack of entrepreneurial enterprise. West Africa possessed no group comparable to the Parsis of India or the Indians of East Africa. Few Africans possessed the capital or know-how necessary to start local ventures. Thus the only likely source of industrial investment was the large trading companies, of whom the Compagnie Française de l'Afrique Occidentale (CFAO), the Société Commerciale de l'Ouest Africain and the subsidiaries of Unilever were the most important. But, although Unilever established a soap factory in Nigeria as early as 1923, in French West Africa none of the trading companies were attracted by the possibility of large-scale industrial investment, except in processing export commodities, until after 1960. Unlike the mining companies in the Congo, these had no large community of employees to serve and their wealth was based partly on the import trade, which local manufacture of consumer goods would reduce.

For these and other reasons industrial development came late and slowly in most parts of the federation. Before 1939 about half the total industry of French West Africa was concentrated at Dakar, the centre of government and the main naval base. These factories fell into two categories: those processing export commodities such as ground-nuts to reduce the costs of freight; and import substituting ventures designed to take advantage of the effective protection provided by the availability of local raw materials or the cost of importing bulky goods. The list included beverages, salt, soap, canned foods, matches, cheap textiles and tobacco. It is impossible to estimate the value of these products before 1939 but it must have been very small. The Second World War and its immediate aftermath, when France was cut off from the colonies and was thus unable to supply them with the goods they needed, provided an immense stimulus to develop these and other consumer industries. After 1950 the reviving French manufacturers attempted to block this development which threatened their export market. But from then on both the big trading companies and some foreign industrial firms, such as the shoe-making company, Bata, of Canada, established subsidiaries in the federation. Moreover for the first time factories were being built in places other than Dakar, mainly in the ports such as Abidjan in the Ivory Coast. Dakar nevertheless retained its industrial preponderance until the federation broke up after 1960: in that year Senegal had 250 factories employing 14,000 workers and this was the only industrial complex in French West Africa.[36]

The effects of this concentrated industrial development on the economy of the federation as a whole are difficult to assess because statistics are inadequate; but some general trends can be outlined. First, from the 1920s there was a marked shift to the processing of primary export commodities, normally the first stage of industrialization in an underdeveloped economy. The 'industrial' share of exports rose from 2 per cent in 1926 to 13 per cent in 1938 and 26 per cent in 1953.[37] By then the greater part of ground-nut exports was either being decorticated or converted into oil. Second, as local industries provided substitutes, consumption goods declined as a proportion of the value of total imports, from 76.2 per cent in 1925 to 53 per cent in 1951, and capital equipment increased from 22.6 per cent of imports in 1929 to 31 per cent in 1955.[38] In the Ivory

Coast the product of industry and construction rose from 5.6 billion francs in 1950 to 15.1 billion in 1960 at constant prices, increasing from 8.7 to 11.4 per cent of the gross domestic product.[39]

Yet, although industrial activity was probably the fastest-growing sector of the economy of the more favoured regions of French West Africa, the actual achievement was limited. Thus while industry and construction provided 11.4 per cent of the gross domestic product there in 1960, they contributed 19.6 per cent in the Congo in 1957, 19.5 per cent in Kenya the same year, 13.4 per cent in Nigeria 1956 and 25 per cent in South Africa in 1957.[40] Manufacturing as such provided only about 2 per cent of the gross domestic product in French Guinea in 1960, compared with 10 per cent in the Congo and in Kenya and 14 per cent in the Central African Federation.[41] Manufacturing still employed a very small proportion of the total population, as in other West African countries. The percentages for 1955 were Nigeria, 0.09 per cent; French West Africa, 0.14 per cent; Gold Coast, 0.44 per cent; Kenya, 0.70 per cent; the Congo, 0.87 per cent. At the end of the colonial period French West Africa had hardly begun to industrialize and the great majority of even those industries that did exist were owned and run by expatriates. Such facts provide strong arguments for those who hold that colonialism was incompatible with 'balanced' economic growth in the dependencies.

Taken in conjunction, these studies of three particular colonial dependencies show that, although achievements varied immensely, it is correct to say that colonialism did not in general result in the transformation of agricultural into industrial economies. The charge of 'lop-sided' economic development cannot be rebutted. Yet it would be equally wrong to attribute this to any one cause, least of all to the fact of colonial rule. Limited industrialization was the result of complex factors, many of them much deeper than the effects of colonialism. On the one hand, very few non-European societies possessed the attitudes, skills or capital necessary to generate mechanized industry on their own account. On the other hand, the imperial powers did little to stimulate industrialization and diversification before about 1945, when these aims were at last adopted by most imperial governments. Empire alone was not the cause of

limited industrial growth but until the last decades of colonialism
it was too readily accepted by the imperial authorities that industry
was a natural growth which must not be forced.

4. Conclusions

Only a dogmatist would attempt to state categorically that colonialism was either totally inconsistent with economic development in
the dependencies or, alternatively, that it was the best possible
medium for stimulating their growth. Colonialism was not sufficiently consistent over time to justify any such sweeping assertions,
nor were its objectives sufficiently coherent to achieve any particular
result.

The time factor is critical because even in the short time-span
between about 1870 and 1945 colonialism changed constantly. In
the early years, to about 1914, the statesmen of Europe, who had
divided the world largely to resolve international frictions that might
have endangered the peace of Europe, found it necessary to justify
the cost of empire to their electorates and to satisfy the demands
of domestic interest groups. The result was the proclaimed aim of
'exploiting' the new possessions in the interest of the metropolis;
and it was this that produced most of the worst features of imperial
policy on land, labour and tariff control that have been outlined
above. Yet this phase did not last long. By the First World War
the conscience of Europe had rebelled and from then until about
1945 the accepted doctrine of empire was the 'dual mandate'. Empire
involved a duty to develop the colonies in the mutual interest of the
local inhabitants and the world economy and moral imperatives
must take priority over economic advantage. This new consensus
resulted in the gradual abolition of the most notorious institutions
of exploitation – the vast concessions, expropriation of native land,
the use of semi-servile labour, etc. But it did not by itself guarantee
much positive action to ameliorate the poverty of colonial societies.
Except in the most politically advanced colonies, such as India, Ceylon and Indonesia, which were for the first time given substantial
freedom to adopt tariff and other policies intended to stimulate local
industry, it was expected that the beneficial forces of the world

market would be sufficient to generate whatever economic growth was feasible. In practice this meant the expansion of colonial economies based on production of export commodities, which in turn suffered severely from the disastrous slump in prices and demand during the slump of the 1930s. Nothing did more to give colonialism a bad name among economists and nationalists, who concluded that industrialization was essential to protect these countries from fluctuations in the international market.

Again this set of assumptions did not last. As the European states themselves adopted protected and 'managed' economies in the 1930s and 1940s, it became accepted that the same techniques must be applied to the colonies. There therefore followed some two decades of 'welfare colonialism' during which the authorities planned vast changes in the colonial economies and began to give or lend, comparatively, very large sums of money to get 'development' under way. Much had been achieved by the varying dates at which the colonies became politically independent; yet it was not enough to make any of them 'developed' or 'rich'. Colonialism thus died before it could demonstrate whether it was capable of converting poor into rich societies.

Colonialism was thus in a state of constant flux. The important point is that economic development carried out before 1945 or even 1960 cannot usefully be compared with that of independent states under the conditions of the 1970s or later, for conditions were not comparable. Before 1939 almost no European state, except the USSR and Nazi Germany, had a fully 'managed' economy. It is therefore unhistorical to speak as if colonialism alone prevented the use of modern management techniques in the colonies. Had these been independent at that time they would almost certainly have followed the same 'liberal' economic policies as the less-developed states of Latin America, with comparably limited results. Colonialism must be judged by the standards of its own time.

Indeed a more useful approach to the economic effects of colonialism is to see it as a factor of limited importance whose main effect was to integrate less-developed societies into the international economy, using whatever techniques of economic control happened to be in vogue at a particular time. That there were strong elements of self-interest in these techniques is not to be denied: the very concept and practice of an 'imperial economy', in which the colonies played whatever role best suited the metropolis, suggests this. Yet the underlying reality was that this allocation of complementary economic roles between an industrialized metropolis and an agricultural dependency would have happened in any case, even without colonialism. As the modern proponents of 'underdevelopment' theory argue, formal colonies were in much the same position as any other less-developed society, even if politically independent. For each the reality was that they were of marginal importance to the centres of international wealth, in somewhat the same way as the poorer agricultural provinces of individual European or North American states were marginal to their own industrial and financial centres. In this sense the world consisted of concentric rings of wealth and power, each differentiated by how much capital and technology it possessed. The most difficult problem at both national and international level was to overcome these natural and historical inequalities. The fact of what Marxists call 'unequal development' has not yet been fully eliminated within either capitalist or socialist states in the West and it is not surprising that it was not successfully dealt with by the colonial powers within their empires.

It would thus appear that colonialism deserves neither the praise nor the blame it has often been given for, if it did relatively little to overcome the causes of poverty in the colonies, neither did it make them poor for the first time. Empire had very significant economic effects, some good, some bad; but nowhere did it fundamentally change the underlying character of colonial society or resolve its problems. In fact, to have done this would have required a degree of determination over a very long time and a volume of resources that no imperial power could ever muster. This is one reason why, after 1945, so many in Europe and the colonies believed that decolonization alone could mark the beginning of a brave new world in the newly liberated dependencies. But they, like the imperialists before them, underestimated the obstacles to development. Despite the unprecedented flood of foreign aid and investment and the considerable efforts made by many ex-colonial governments to get sustained economic gowth under way, the countries of Africa, Asia and Latin America remained in the later 1970s as poor in relation to the rich countries of Europe and North America as they had been in

1945 or even in 1870. If the imperialists had failed to develop the 'third world' effectively it was still uncertain whether their sovereign successors could do much better.

Notes

1. Adam Smith, *The Wealth of Nations*, (Everyman edition, London 1966), vol. II, p. 89.

2. Karl Marx, *Capital*, (Chicago 1909), vol. III, p. 279.

3. W. Rodney, *How Europe Underdeveloped Africa*, (London and Dar es Salaam 1972), p. 256.

4. Lord Lugard, *The Dual Mandate in British Tropical Africa*, (1922, 3rd ed. London 1926), p. 509.

5. See his *Afrique noire: l'ère coloniale*, (Paris 1964) for the best exposition of the 'immiseration' thesis on French West Africa.

6. I. Little, T. Scitovsky and M. Scott, *Industry and Trade in some Developing Countries*, (London 1970), table 5.2, p. 174.

7. For a more detailed critical account of this question see B.R. Tomlinson, *The Political Economy of the Raj, 1914–1947*, (London 1979).

8. For a study of Italian state enterprise see C. Segre, *Fourth Shore. The Italian Colonization of Libya*, (Chicago 1974).

9. On the Chinese in South-east Asia see V. Purcell, *The Chinese in South-East Asia*, (London 1951, 2nd ed. 1965). On Indian migration see H. Tinker, *A New System of Slavery*, (London 1974).

10. Quoted in C.H. Wilson, *The History of Unilever*, (2 vols London 1954), vol. II, pp. 166–7.

11. For British territories in Africa there is a useful summary in L.P. Mair, *Native Policies in Africa*, (London 1936). See also M. Perham, *Native Administration in Nigeria*, (London 1937) and Lord Hailey, *Native Administration in the British African Territories*, (5 vols London 1950–53). For French territories see A. Girault, *Principes de Colonisation et de Législation coloniale*, (Paris 1927–33), P.F. Gonidec, *Droit d'Outre-Mer*, (2 vols Paris 1959), and J. Suret-Canale, *Afrique noire: l'ère coloniale*.

12. There is an account of HCB in D.K. Fieldhouse, *Unilever Overseas*, (London 1978), ch. 9.

13. See Daniel Thorner in *The Times*, (London) 9 September 1968.

14. G. Blyn, *Agricultural Trends in India, 1891–1947*, (Philadelphia 1966) pp. 104, 151. The accuracy of these statistics has, however, been questioned. See Clive Dewey, '*Patwar:* and *Chaukidar*: Subordinate Officials and the Reliability of India's Agricultural Statistics', in *The Imperial Impact: Studies in the Economic History of Africa and India* ed. C. Dewey and A.G. Hopkins, (London 1978), pp. 280–314.

15. J. Suret-Canale, *L'ère coloniale*, p. 371.

16. J.–J. Poquin, *Les Relations Economiques Extérieures du Pays d'Afrique noire de l'Union Française, 1925–55*, (Paris 1957) p. 134.

17. J. Suret-Canale, *L'ère coloniale*, p. 231.

18. Ibid., p. 213.

19. Ibid., pp. 237–8.

20. A.K. Sen, 'The Commodity Pattern of British Enterprise in early Indian Industrialization, 1854–1914', *Second International Conference of Economic History*, (1962, Paris 1965), pp. 781–803.

21. See for example on Africa, A.G. Hopkins, *An Economic History of West Africa*, (London 1973), P. Kilby, *Industrialization in an Open Economy*, (Cambridge 1969); on India, M. Kidron, *Foreign Investments in India*, (London 1965), D.H. Buchanan, *The Development of Capitalist Enterprise in India*, (1934, 2nd ed. London 1966), A.M. Bagchi, *Private Investment in India, 1900–1939*, (Cambridge 1972); on the Belgian Congo, F. Bézy, *Problèmes structurels de l'économie Congolaise* (Louvain 1957), J.-L. Lacroix, *Industrialisation au Congo*, (Paris 1966), G. Vandewalle, *De conjuncturele evolutie in Kongo en Ruanda-Urundi van 1920 tot 1939 en van 1949 tot 1958*, (Antwerp 1966).

22. For the rise of the Indian cotton industry see Buchanan, *The Development of Capitalist Enterprise;* Bagchi, *Private Investment*; Kidron, *Foreign Investment;* M.D. Morris, *The Emergence of an Indian Labour Force*, (Berkeley and Los Angeles 1965).

23. For the jute industry see Buchanan, op. cit., Bagchi op. cit., A. Dasgupta, 'The Jute Textile Industry', in *Economic History of India, 1857–1956*, ed. V.B. Singh, (Bombay 1965), pp. 260–80.

24. Buchanan, op. cit. p. 254; Kidron, op. cit. p. 10.

25. V. Anstey, *The Economic Development of India*, (4th ed. London 1952), p. 535; H.K. Mazumdar, *Business Saving in India*, (Bombay 1959), p. 140.

26. See for example Bagchi, *Private Enterprise*, pp. 440–3.

27. Lacroix, *Industrialisation au Congo*, pp. 26–9.

28. J. Lefebvre, *Structures économiques du Congo Belge et du Ruanda-Urundi*, (Brussels 1955), p. 61.

29. Lacroix, op. cit., pp, 21–5.

30. Vandewalle, op. cit., pp. 39, 118.

31. Ibid., p. 128.

32. Lacroix, op. cit., p. 106.

33. Lacroix, op. cit., ch. 3.

34. P. Joye and R. Lewin, *Les Trusts au Congo*, (Brussels 1961), p. 103.

35. For a general survey of this topic see Joye and Lewin, op. cit., pp. 203 ff.

36. S. Amin, *Neo-Colonialism in West Africa*, (Harmondsworth 1973), p. 17.

37. Poquin, op. cit., p. 78.

38. Ibid., pp. 78, 88.

39. S. Amin, *Le Développement du capitalisme en Côte d'Ivoire*, (Paris 1967), p. 297.

40. *Economic Survey of Africa since 1950*, (New York 1959), pp. 16–17.

41. E.A.G. Robinson (ed.) *Economic Development for Africa South of the Sahara* (London and New York 1964), p. 12.

III. The Historiography of Modern Colonialism 1870-1945

1. Changing approaches to colonialism

All historical writing is conditioned by the period in which it is written and the preoccupation of the historian. Like the pilot of an aeroplane as it takes off, the early writer starts with a restricted view of a very limited area and his main concern is with immediate problems. As he gains height and safety his range of vision widens, but he can still see houses and fields in great detail and feels directly connected with them. The higher he rises the wider his vision and the greater his detachment from the ground, until eventually he can see the broad shape of the land and even the curvature of the earth. The evolution of historical writing on modern colonialism follows something of the same pattern and can similarly be divided into three periods covering the hundred years after 1870. The first period was contemporary with the early exploration and original occupation of what were to become new colonial territories from 1870–1914. The second evolved as the colonial systems became stabilized between 1914 and 1945. The third followed during and after the period of decolonization from 1945 to the present. Each of these generations of writers had its own characteristic approach to the subject, conditioned by its relationship to current problems and realities, and the books they wrote had distinctive merits and defects. This chapter will therefore start with a short survey of the main features of historical writing on colonialism in each of these periods and will then, in Part 2, list the most important books on each main colonial system in turn.

i. The pioneers before 1914

By no means all parts of the modern colonial empires were annexed for the first time during the later nineteenth century: major possessions, such as British India, Ceylon (Sri Lanka), the Netherlands

Indies (Indonesia) and colonies in the Caribbean had been under European rule for a century or longer by that time. For these places the pioneering era of descriptive and historical writing that was starting on the new colonial territories in Africa and the East was already in the past. A considerable literature on their religions, culture and history already existed, and much of this was characteristic of work later done on the newer colonies during the period after 1914. Thus what follows relates primarily to the 'new' colonies of the later nineteenth century.

The later nineteenth century was a receptive age for published accounts of the first stages of European activity in the newly discovered and soon to be occupied territories. There was a large literate public, fascinated by the romantic aspects of exploration, and printing was cheap. As a result there is a very substantial literature, much of it consisting of articles in journals and newspapers as well as books, about this first era of modern colonialism. The nature and quality of this work varied immensely, but for the modern reader much of the earliest writing, particularly that done before the scramble for political control introduced a new sense of nationalistic bias, has the special virtue that these writers had no particular drum to beat. Many of them reported the scene as they saw it, much as navigators such as James Cook had done a century earlier or as the first astronauts were to do when they reached the moon. This makes this early work of critical importance for the modern historian, for in many cases his knowledge of pre-colonial conditions, particularly in non-literate societies, depends on the accounts left by the first Europeans, supported now by indigenous oral tradition and by archaeology. The characteristic limitation of such studies is, of course, that most of them were by amateurs who had no training in the then newly-born and still very primitive science of anthropology. As a result their descriptions tend to resemble two-dimensional snapshots. They could report on what they saw; but when they attempted to explain the character of the non-European societies they observed they were likely to provide unsatisfactory answers. The modern historian has thus to be very careful how he uses this essential early literature.

Writers of this early generation fall into perhaps four overlapping groups. The earliest in time were the explorers and geographers who first penetrated Africa, parts of Asia and the Pacific and who described what they saw there. This tradition, of course, dates back to the sixteenth century and even before: Marco Polo's epic travels in the East in the late fourteenth century were some of the earliest explorations to be recorded and widely publicized. But in the nineteenth century the establishment of geographical societies in most European capitals (Paris in 1821, Britain in 1828, Berlin in 1830, Italy in 1867) and the existence of scientific societies resulted in much support for explorers and wide diffusion of their findings. The result was a spate of published accounts of the societies and the countries they investigated.

Closely related to the explorers were the missionaries, some of whom, like David Livingstone, were also pioneer explorers. But the missionaries often differed from the explorers in two respects. First, they might stay in a particular place for a long time and thus came to have a much more detailed knowledge of the societies in which they worked. Second, their accounts were more likely to be biased by distaste for certain aspects of these 'pagan' societies which it was their business to transform. But some missionaries were also good scholars and much of their writings is of great importance.

Explorers and missionaries were followed by the first generation of European soldiers and officials and their writing constitutes a second category. These men had an axe to grind: they were there to impose alien rule and suppress native resistance. Hence many of the reports they published were biased against those they conquered and governed. Yet among them were many able and highly educated men; and since they also commonly stayed in one place for a considerable time, they had the opportunity to become reasonably expert in local history and culture. Men such as Sir Harry Johnstone, who played a major role in the creation of British Africa, and J.S. Galliéni, who was a leading French soldier and then administrator in Africa, wrote highly intelligent and balanced accounts of their work and of the indigenous peoples with whom they came into contact. This tradition of scholarly work by colonial officials continued throughout the colonial period and resulted in some of the most important studies that will be mentioned later.

Finally, during this first period before 1914, there arose the first generation of critical writers who were not, as a rule, directly involved in the process of exploration or empire-building, but who were deeply interested in it as observers. On one extreme such men included the French economist and journalist Paul Leroy-Beaulieu who, in 1874, published the first of many editions of his book, *De la Colonisation chez les Peuples modernes*, a vast survey of European colonizing achievements past and present, whose main purpose was to demonstrate the value of French rule both to France and to the colonial peoples. By 1914 there were a number of comparable studies, both general and specific to particular territories. Their evidential basis was limited but they provided a first rough sketch of the origins of European rule and of the character of the new colonies on which later generations could build. At the other end of the spectrum there was an increasing number of observers and writers who, unlike Leroy-Beaulieu, were extremely critical of imperialism and who wrote passionately against it. Probably the best known of these was the British journalist J.A. Hobson. His book, *Imperialism: a Study*, first published in 1902, summarized and developed the arguments then being used by liberals in Britain and elsewhere to show that imperialism and colonial rule were bad both for the imperial states and for the new subject peoples. This book had many later editions and still excites respect and controversy. By 1914 the volume of anti-imperialist literature was considerable and most of the basic economic, moral and sociological grounds on which colonialism was later to be attacked had been defined. The publication of V.I. Lenin's *Imperialism, the Highest Stage of Capitalism* in 1916 provided the European left with what proved to be its bible on all aspects of imperialism and colonialism for the next half century. Like much of the early historical writing these polemical books were based on slender and often inaccurate factual material, but this had little effect on their influence, then or later.

ii. The classical age of colonialism, 1914–1945

The thirty years after 1914 saw two parallel developments: colonial rule became highly professionalized and at the same time the literature achieved a degree of maturity as those who wrote about the colonies acquired fuller understanding of the subject. In this period there were two main categories of authors writing on colonialism: the professional colonial administrators and the scholars.

The first two decades after 1920 saw a spate of writing by men with experience of running the colonies, stimulated by the demand for books to be used by the growing number of men training for the colonial services. For the most part their aims were didactic – to argue a particular view of the purpose of empire and how it should be run – or propagandist – to popularize the concept of empire and to persuade the public at home that colonialism was justified and worthwhile. Writers in the first category were particularly concerned with the hotly debated issue (outlined in Chapter I) on how the new colonies should be administered. On the British side the most influential writer was Lord Lugard who, after long service in British Africa, published his book, *The Dual Mandate in British Tropical Africa*, in 1922 as a manifesto of the principle of indirect rule through indigenous chiefs rather than through direct intervention by European officials and native paid auxiliaries. Lugard stimulated a considerable body of literature during the following twenty years, of which two of the best-known works were Dame Margery Perham's *Native Administration in Nigeria* (1937) and Sir D. Cameron's *My Tanganyika Service and Some Nigeria* (1939). Both these supported Lugard, but after about 1940 later writers became increasingly critical of his ideas. In France the old concept of 'assimilation' was discredited by 1914 and the currently fashionable doctrine between the wars was 'association', which one French administrator later described as 'Lugardism that was moderate, anaemic'. The classical expression of official French attitudes to colonialism between the wars was *La Mise en Valeur des Colonies Françaises* (1923) by Albert Sarraut, Colonial Minister during most of the 1920s, which argued that under colonialism the interests of France and her colonies could be fully reconciled provided France spent a great deal for the first time on colonial development. Most of the considerable volume of French official writings on colonialism in this period followed Sarraut's general argument, paying lip-service to Lugard, but never adopting his strict principles for administration.

More valuable to the modern student are the substantial scholarly historical writings of colonial officials, sometimes done after retirement. On the British side the publication of the *Cambridge History*

of India, much of it written by present or past members of the Indian
Civil Service, reflected the high intellectual standards of that Service
and the long tradition that Indian administrators should become
experts in the history, culture and languages of the subcontinent.
The *Cambridge History of the British Empire*, all but one of whose
volumes were published by 1945 and which included two volumes
of the *History of India*, was very important because it provided the
first general account in any detail of British imperial history to about
1914. But it had one important limitation: there was no volume on
Africa and very little on Africa in the general volumes. The reason
was that historical research on that continent was still in its infancy
and few members of the Colonial Service aspired to the same scholarly ambitions as Indian Civilians. It is, in fact, significant that the
first methodical study of conditions and problems in British colonial
Africa was made by an ex-Indian Civilian, Lord Hailey, whose ency-
clopedic *An African Survey* was first published in 1938. Other shorter
books written by Britons with official experience included Sir
G. V. Fiddes' *The Dominions and Colonial Offices*, Sir M. C. C. Seton's
The India Office (both published in 1926 as part of the same series
on British administrative departments) and Lord Olivier's *Jamaica,
the Blessed Isle* (1936), of which he had been governor. French officialdom was equally active in providing accounts of the empire it
was responsible for. In 1926 Albert Duchêne, a former official of
the Colonial Ministry, published a pioneer study of the evolution
of that ministry under the title *La Politique coloniale de la France*,
and followed this with *Histoire des Frances coloniales de la France*
in 1938. Georges Hardy, formerly director of the Ecole Coloniale
at Paris, published a *Histoire sociale de la Colonisation française* in
1935. The Ecole stimulated a substantial number of books to be used
by students who were required to understand the complex laws and
usages on which the French empire was based: hence this was a category of studies which has no exact equivalent in British literature
on colonialism because the British empire was far less legalistic in
character. Most important was A. Girault's *Principes de Colonisation
et de Législation coloniale*, which reached its fourth edition in 1927–
30. Among many other similar studies was *Législation et Finances
coloniales* by L. Rolland (ed.), published in 1930.

Studies of this type by men directly concerned with colonial affairs merged imperceptibly into works by scholars. By the 1920s the colonial empires were old enough and aroused sufficient academic interest (particularly among students hoping to qualify for imperial appointments) to stimulate serious academic work. The main handicap at this time was that the official records were not yet open: in Britain the Public Record Office and India Office Library were both subject to a fifty-year rule, so that by 1945 scholars still had access only to material up to 1895, which was before most of the new colonies were fully established. Historians had thus to rely mainly on printed official and other sources, though anthropologists, who used field work and oral evidence, were not handicapped in the same way. As a result few serious historical studies published in this period, however well done, can still be regarded as authoritative; but some at least laid down the lines of debate that have lasted into the 1970s. On the British empire probably the most influential work published between the two wars was Sir Keith Hancock's three volume series *Survey of British Commonwealth Affairs* (1937–42) which opened up new and fruitful lines of enquiry into many parts of the empire, including both the self-governing dominions such as Canada and also tropical Africa. Also of seminal importance were Sir Reginald Coupland's two volumes on East Africa: *East Africa and its Invaders* (1938) and *The Exploitation of East Africa, 1856–1890* (1939). Contemporary interest in the economic development of the colonies was reflected in two other pioneering works: A. McPhee's *The Economic Revolution in West Africa* (1926) and L.C.A. Knowles' *The Economic Development of the British Overseas Empire* (3 vols 1924–36). Both emphasized the innovative role of Europeans in the colonies and largely ignored the importance of indigenous modes of production and exchange; but these remained the standard works until the 1960s. Equally important on a topic of great contemporary concern was R.L. Buell's *The Native Problem in Africa* (1928) which dealt with problems of race, labour and administration in British, French and Belgian territories south of the Sahara from the standpoint of an independent American observer. Other still valuable books written in this period were R. Emerson's *Malaysia: a Study in Direct and Indirect Rule* (1937) and L.A. Mills' *Ceylon under British Rule, 1795–1932* (1933).

In France also this period saw the publication of a number of large works by scholars who laid the foundations for a more critical and detailed study of the French colonial empire later on. The largest single collection was the six volume work edited by G. Hanotaux and A. Martineau, *Histoire des Colonies françaises et de l'expansion de la France dans le monde*. This was a semi-popular account, heavily patriotic in tone. Another corporate work in four volumes was published by the Union Coloniale Française between 1929 and 1930 called *Le Domaine colonial français*. A more durable and academic study edited by Ch.-A. Julien, *Les Techniciens de la Colonisation*, was published in 1945. Meantime several influential, though now dated, studies of French colonialism had been published in English: S. H. Roberts' *History of French Colonial Policy, 1870–1925* (2 vols 1929); H. I. Priestley's *France Overseas* (1938); and C. Southworth's *The French Colonial Venture* (1931) which set out to show that, in economic and financial terms, the French empire was a net financial burden on the metropolis.

By 1945 a serious historical literature was also beginning to grow up on the smaller colonial empires. The Netherlands Indies aroused the greatest interest overseas, mainly because of the Dutch emphasis on 'indirect' methods of government. A. D. A. De Kat Angelino published the English version of his *Colonial Policy* in two volumes in 1931 and this had considerable influence. It was followed in 1939 by *Netherlands India* by J. S. Furnivall, a British colonial official who had served in Burma and who compared Dutch practice favourably with that of Britain. His later book, *Colonial Policy and Practice* (1948) had great influence in Britain during the period of decolonization. Other studies were A. Vandenbosch, *The Dutch East Indies* (3rd ed. 1944); G. H. Bouquet, *A French View of the Netherlands Indies* (English translation, 1940); and B. H. M. Vlekke's *Nusantara. A History of the East Indian Archipelago* (1944). These contained a considerable amount of common information and it was clear by the early 1940s that more basic research was necessary before the history of the Dutch possessions could go much further.

Much less scholarly work had been done on the Belgian Congo (Zaïre), other than in official handbooks, journals, etc. Indeed, until the 1920s the most influential work was probably still that of E. D. Morel, an Englishman, whose scathing attack on the system of rule under Leopold II in his *King Leopold's Rule in Africa* (1904) and in later works on the same period still provided the standard view of recent Congo history; though A.J.Wauters, a Belgian geographer, had published a more moderate *Histoire du Congo Belge* in 1911. By 1945, however, this gap had been partly filled. On the official side Pierre Ryckmans, then Governor-General of the Congo, published *La Politique coloniale* which was comparable as a manifesto for a morally defensible imperial system with the work of Lugard and Sarraut. The two most important scholarly studies were L.Franck's *Le Congo Belge* (2 vols 1923) and G. Van De Kerken's *La Politique coloniale Belge* (Antwerp 1943), which between them laid the foundations for the modern historiography of the Congo.

In 1945, however, there was still very little good historical work available on the other empires. Perhaps stimulated by the Pacific war after 1942 American scholars, who had taken a leading part in writing about other empires, produced some competent studies of their own possessions. J.W. Pratt had already published a durable study of *The Expansionists of 1898* in 1936. On individual colonies there was J.R. Hayden's *The Philippines* (1942), W.C. Forbes' *The Philippine Islands* (rev. ed. 1945) and S.K. Stevens' *American Expansion in Hawaii, 1842–1898* (1945). Much less had been published on the Portuguese possessions other than official propaganda and treatises on law and administration. G.Do C. Ribeiro's *Historia Colonial* (2 vols 1937–8) was probably the most valuable popular account; but there was still no useful book in English on the modern period and very little fundamental research had yet been done. On the short-lived German empire, destroyed in 1919, the German argument between the wars that her colonies should be returned had generated a considerable literature, much of it favourable to Germany. The official line was provided by a former colonial governor, A.H. Schnee, in *German Colonization Past and Future* (Eng. trs. 1921). There were also the first of what later became a large number of scholarly studies. A.J.P. Taylor's *Germany's First Bid for Colonies, 1884–85* (1938) was a serious research work based on original sources. M.E. Townsend's *Origins of Modern German Colonialism, 1871–85* (1921) and *The Rise and Fall of Germany's Colonial Empire, 1884–1918* (1930) were largely based on printed sources and do not now carry conviction; but they provided a useful introduction and formed the basis of later critical analysis. H.R. Rudin's *Germans in the Cameroons, 1884–1914* (1938) was a pioneering 'revisionist' book using original materials which showed the way for similar studies made after 1945. Finally Italy's active expansionist and colonizing enterprises during the 1920s and 1930s stimulated a number of studies. Many were frankly propaganda, but there were some serious and durable publications which, although not based on original sources, laid foundations for more scholarly studies later on.

Thus a general comment on the state of the historiography of modern colonialism by 1945 might be that for most colonial empires there was now a reasonably comprehensive literature which covered most territories and provided a ground-plan for later research. Despite wide variations in quality and approach there were two common limitations. First, because most official records were not available, much of the analysis of official intentions was necessarily conjectural. Second, the fact that empire was a continuing reality and that colonial policy was highly controversial tended to colour even scholarly writing. The common underlying assumption of most writers (apart from the minority of radical critics of colonialism) was that empire was both actually and potentially of benefit to metropolis and colonies alike, that it would last for an indefinite period, and that the main need was for more careful analysis of the 'right' method of running an empire. Since past experience was thought to be a good guide to future conduct, much of even the best literature still had a didactic tone, and this distinguishes it from most of the work done after the 1950s when decolonization at last left the scholar free to study colonial history without prior commitment.

iii. 1945–1980

The basic fact about the historical literature on colonialism is that by far the great majority of serious and now acceptable books were published after 1945 and that their number is still growing fast. Indeed, there are now so many that it would be impossible in a small space to make any useful comment on even the most important of them. How does one account for this immense increase in both the quality and quantity of books on colonialism?

For the improvement in quality, particularly of academic studies, there seem to have been two main reasons. First, the process of time and the relaxation in the rule concerning the use of official material in a number of countries (notably Britain, which reduced the 'quarantine period' to thirty years in the 1960s) has by now resulted in the records being open until the later 1940s. This in turn enables the historian to write with confidence. Of equal significance is the fact that colonial history at last achieved respectability in the academic community. Between the wars colonialism was regarded as marginal to standard history syllabuses at most universities, partly because there were so few good books on it and also because it was assumed, with some justification, to have too utilitarian a purpose – to train future colonial administrators. After 1945, and still more from the 1960s, this taint disappeared as the colonial empires were disbanded: in death they acquired respectability as a subject for academic study. Colonial history could now be treated from a secular standpoint, either as part of the history of the European metropolitan states or in terms of the history of individual ex-colonial states.

An important contributory factor, which also affected the way in which modern colonial history came to be written, was the great increase after 1945 in the number and quality of universities in the colonies and then ex-colonies. This development was initially a product of the post-war concern of the main imperial powers to offset nascent movements for colonial independence by improving conditions of all sorts and in particular to counter the accusation that they did not make it possible for their colonial subjects to achieve adequate levels of education without going overseas. In the early years the new universities were necessarily staffed largely by Europeans who naturally concentrated their historical research on local topics on which there were materials available. As a result some of the most valuable studies of British and French colonies written in the 1950s and early 1960s were by British and French expatriates. Moreover, because they were using local materials, their emphasis tended to be placed on the autonomous history of a particular territory and to be seen from the point of view of its inhabitants, whereas most previous colonial history had been written in terms of the achievements of the imperial powers with the leading roles played by Europeans. This trend towards 'area' studies was probably the most important single development in this period. Pioneered by

Europeans, it was quickly taken up by the first generations of indigenous scholars, who naturally tended to see colonialism as an external influence on their own societies and applied quite different interpretations to it. This was the root of many of the very detailed monographs now available on particular regions or countries and in most respects it must be regarded as a valuable new development. The only reservation to be made is that if the 'area' approach is taken too far it may result in an underestimate of the importance of the imperial influence during the period of colonialism. This is to distort history in the same way as in the past imperial historians distorted it by laying too much stress on the role played by Europeans rather than by their subject peoples.

One consequence of this new interest in the autonomous history of the colonial territories was a search for indigenous source materials as an addition or alternative to the conventional European sources. The main problem faced by the new historians was that many pre-colonial societies, particularly in Africa and the Pacific, had not been literate, so that no conventional written records of the past were available. Even in literate societies the surviving sources were likely to be restricted to the business of the government or the records of religious bodies whose literacy was greatest. Researchers therefore increasingly used and relied on oral evidence, along with archaeology, both to push back the limits of knowledge beyond the date at which European materials were available and also to provide an 'alternative' interpretation of events to that written by Europeans. Not all such work carried equal conviction, since oral tradition has serious limitations; but at least this approach helped to correct what had undoubtedly been a serious imbalance in the history of colonialism when it was written entirely from European sources.

These developments help to account for both the higher quality and increased output of post-1945 work on colonialism. Paradoxically the volume of publications was greatly stimulated by the decline and fall of the empires themselves. This can be seen in three main ways at various times. First, for perhaps a decade after 1945, although the bulk of the Asian and North African colonies were now independent, it was still generally assumed that most of the African, Pacific and Caribbean colonies were likely to remain dependencies for a considerable period. At the same time it was obvious that fundamental change of all kinds was essential if the colonial peoples, now more than ever before conscious of their subordinate position, were to be persuaded that it was in their interests to accept the fact of continuing colonialism. The result was a period of what has been described above as 'welfare colonialism' which entailed much closer imperial involvement in the domestic affairs of the colonies than ever before; and this in turn created demand for more detailed information about them. This demand stimulated scholars; and although some of their work was obviously affected by current controversies over methods of government and economic development, much of it was also academically valuable.

Meantime a second new incentive for research had developed. As it became evident that the time-table for devolution of power from the imperial metropolis to the dependencies would have to be much faster than had at first been envisaged, interest in the origins and character of the 'patriotic', 'nationalist' or 'resistance' movements which were obviously stimulating the imperial powers to wind up their empires grew rapidly. The result was a whole new literature on the genesis of such movements which involved investigation into both non-European attitudes to alien rule and into those European policies which might have been responsible for growing alienation among the subject peoples. Such studies fitted well with the new interest in indigenous local history that has been mentioned above and also attracted specialists from disciplines other than history, such as political theorists and anthropologists. Moreover this emphasis on the role of indigenous 'nationalists' served their purposes very well because it tended to dignify them and their objectives; and once they had achieved independence, the writing of interpretations of the colonial past from this standpoint was stimulated by the need of each new state to possess its own 'national' history. Some of the books published in and after the 1960s along these lines verged on myth-making; yet there was also much valuable work done and on the whole concern with the genesis of nationalist consciousness can be seen as a constructive stimulus to historians both in Europe and overseas.

The third stimulus to research and writing on colonialism after 1945 came from the aftermath of decolonization. It has been seen above that before 1914 there was a considerable and highly influential literature produced by opponents or critics of imperialism who commonly imputed imperial expansion and colonialism to the economic needs of the capitalist countries. Colonies, in fact, were acquired so that they could be 'exploited'. Between 1916 (Lenin's *Imperialism*) and 1945 these ideas continued to form the basis of left-wing and socialist attitudes to colonialism; yet there was a remarkable lack of new ideas or books analysing the economic relations between Europe and the colonies from a Marxist point of view. The left generally accepted the truth of Lenin's argument and felt that there was little that could be added to it. Individuals, such as André Gide, who published accounts of conditions in French colonies (his *Voyage au Congo*, 1927, and *Le Retour du Tchad*, 1928, were serious indictments of French activities in these regions) might attempt to demonstrate the fact of exploitation, but no one seems to have thought it necessary or possible to develop Lenin's approach further. Above all it was assumed that economic exploitation of the colonies would end with colonialism and that colonialism would automatically end when capitalism itself was destroyed in Europe and North America.

But when decolonization came in the two decades after 1945 it did not result from the fall of capitalism throughout the world; nor did political independence seem necessarily to end foreign control and exploitation of the one-time colonies. This fact had much the same stimulating effect on European Marxists and socialists as the partition of the world had done in the decades after 1880: it forced them to produce a new theory concerning the roots of poverty in the one-time colonies, which is commonly called the theory of neo-colonialism described in Chapter I. The new approach can perhaps be dated from the publication of P.A. Baran's *The Political Economy of Growth* in 1957. Thereafter the basic assumption of the many who contributed to what came to be called 'dependency' or 'underdevelopment' literature was that the underlying relationship between Europe and North America on the one hand and the less-developed countries on the other was economic rather than political. So long as the rich states remained capitalist it did not matter much whether the poor countries were technically colonies or independent states: either way they were bound to take a subordinate position as 'satellites' of the rich states because their economies were structured to serve the interests of international capitalism, either as producers of raw materials or as consumers of imported manufactures. It followed that the process of political decolonization might have no significance in economic or social terms unless the new states used their freedom to renounce capitalism and all economic contact with the capitalist states.

This argument was primarily polemical: it was part of the conflict of ideas between the capitalist West and the socialist East. Most of the literature was therefore theoretical. Yet one strand of the theory acted as a stimulant to historians of colonialism. The proponents of dependency theory argued that the historical role of colonialism had been to complete the incorporation of the less-developed countries into the international capitalist economy and that in the process these colonies had been made 'poor' for the first time by the imperial powers. This at least raised an issue of fact which gave scope for historical research. In the 1970s public interest in the controversy had the effect of stimulating a considerable amount of work on the evolution of colonial economies and social systems whose aim was either to prove or disprove the assertion that the poverty of the modern 'third world' was an invariable and necessary consequence of colonialism in the past.

A broad overview of the evolution of the literature on modern colonialism supports the conclusion, perhaps a platitude, that at every stage those who wrote about it, in common with those writing about all other countries at all times, were conditioned by the current preoccupations of their own age. Before 1914 there was little serious historical writing on the recently acquired colonies, though some valuable work was done on the more distant colonial past; at the same time the main lines of dogmatic controversy concerning the character of imperialism and colonialism were firmly laid by critics and supporters of colonization, arguing in most cases from prejudice rather than from accurate information. Between 1914 and 1945 the foundations of modern academic history of the colonies were laid; but limitation of the source material available and the need to establish the basic outlines of past events had the result that few detailed studies of individual territories were published and there was a tendency to concentrate on contentious issues such as the best method of governing the colonies. Finally, during the decades after 1945 when colonialism reached its end, the study of its history at last achieved maturity and respectability. In the later 1970s the flood of books and articles was still accelerating; and the selective bibliography that follows will necessarily appear outdated within a very short time.

2. A short bibliography of modern colonialism

I. The theory and practice of modern colonialism

1. General surveys and bibliographies

Betts, R.F., *Europe Overseas* (New York 1968).

Blet, H., *France d'Outre-Mer* vol. III, *L'œûvre coloniale de la Troisième République* (Grenoble 1950).

Bridges, R.C. and others (eds), *Nations and Empires: Documents on the History of Europe and its Relation with the World since 1648* (London 1969).

Brunschwig, H., *La Colonisation française* (Paris 1949).

Deschamps, H., *Les Méthodes et Doctrines coloniales de la France* (Paris 1953).

Fieldhouse, D.K., *The Colonial Empires* (London 1966).

Frank, André G., *Dependent Accumulation and Underdevelopment* (London 1978).

Ganiage, J., *L'expansion Coloniale de la France sous la Troisième République* (Paris 1968).

Gillard, D., *The Struggle for Asia, 1828–1914* (London 1977).

Girault, A., *The Colonial Tariff Policy of France* (Oxford 1916).

Gonidec, P.F., *Droit d'Outre-Mer* (2 vols Paris 1959).

Halstead, J.P. and S. Porcari, *Modern European Imperialism: a Bibliography of Books and Articles* (Boston 1974).

Hardy, G., *La Politique coloniale et le Partage de la Terre* (Paris 1937).

McIntyre, W.D. *The Commonwealth of Nations: Origins and Impact, 1869–1971* (Minneapolis 1977).

Mansergh, N., *The Commonwealth Experience* (London 1969).

Porter, B.J., *The Lion's Share: A Short History of British Imperialism, 1850–1970* (London 1976).

Roberts, S.H., *The History of French Colonial Policy 1870–1925* (2 vols London 1929).

Robinson, K., *The Dilemmas of Trusteeship* (London 1965).

Sedillot, R., *Histoire des colonisations* (Paris 1958).

Winks, R.W. (ed.), *The Historiography of the British Empire – Commonwealth* (Durham N.C. 1966).

2. Colonialism and economic development: practice and theory

Baran, P., *The Political Economy of Growth* (New York 1962).

Bauer, P.T., *Dissent on Development: Studies and Debates in Development Economics* (London 1971).

Bloch-Lainé, F., *La Zone Franc* (Paris 1956).

Brown, M. B., *After Imperialism* (London 1963).

Clark, G., *The Balance Sheets of Imperialism* (New York 1936).

Coats, A.W. (ed.), *The Classical Economists and Economic Policy* (London 1971).

Conan, A.R., *The Sterling Area* (London 1952).

Drummond, I.M., *British Economic Policy and the Empire 1919–1939* (London 1972).

Ehrhard, J., *Le Destin du Colonialisme* (Paris, 1957).

Fanon, F., *Dying Colonialism* (New York 1959).

Fanon, F., *The Wretched of the Earth* (New York 1966).

Fay, C.R., *Imperial Economy* (Oxford 1934).

Feis, H., *Europe, the World's Banker 1870–1914* (New York 1961).

Freyssinet, J., *Le Concept de Sous-Développement* (Paris 1966).

Hall, A.R. (ed.), *The Export of Capital from Britain 1870–1914* (London 1969).

Hancock, W.K., *Survey of British Commonwealth Affairs* vol. II, *Problems of Economic Policy 1918–1939*, parts I and II (London 1940–42).

Healy, D., *Modern Imperialism: Changing Styles in Historical Interpretation* (Washington 1967).

Hobson, J.A., *Imperialism: a Study* (London 1902).

Hynes, W.G., *The Economics of Empire, Africa and the New Imperialism 1870–1895* (London 1979).

Imlah, A.H., *Economic Elements in the Pax Britannica* (Cambridge Mass. 1958).

Kay, G.B., *The Political Economy of Colonialism in Ghana; A Collection of Documents and Statistics, 1900–1960* (Cambridge 1972).

Kemp, T., *Theories of Imperialism* (London 1967).

Langley, M., *Britain's Africa* (London 1971).

Lenin, V.I., *Imperialism, the Highest Stage of Capitalism* (Moscow 1917).

Levin, J.V., *The Export Economies* (Cambridge Mass. 1960).

Leys, C., *Underdevelopment in Kenya: The Political Economy of Neo-Colonialism, 1964–71* (London 1975).

Mandel, E., *Marxist Economic Theory* (London 1968).

Mannoni, D.O., *Prospero and Caliban: The Psychology of Colonialization* (New York 1964).

Meier, G.M., *International Trade and Development* (New York 1963).

Meyer, F.V., *Britain's Colonies in World Trade* (London 1948).
Myint, H., *Economic Theory and the Underdeveloped Countries* (Oxford 1971).
Myrdal, G., *Economic Theory and Underdeveloped Regions* (London 1957).
Nurkse, R., *Patterns of Trade and Development* (Stockholm 1959).
O'Connor, J., *The Meaning of Economic Imperialism* (Ann Arbor Mich. 1968).
Owen, R. and R. Sutcliffe (eds), *Studies in the Theory of Imperialism* (London 1972).
Porter, B., *Critics of Empire: British Radical Attitudes to Colonialism in Africa 1895–1914* (London 1968).
Rodney, W., *How Europe Underdeveloped Africa* (London 1972).
Sarraut, A., *La Mise en valeur des Colonies françaises* (Paris 1923).
Southworth, C., *The French Colonial Venture* (London 1931).
Stahl, K.M., *The Metropolitan Orgaization of British Colonial Trade* (London 1951).
Swezy, P.M., *The Theory of Capitalist Development* (London 1946).
White, H.D., *The French International Accounts* (Cambridge Mass. 1933).
Winslow, E.M., *The Pattern of Imperialism* (New York 1948).

II. Colonialism in Africa

1. General surveys

Allen, C. and R.W. Johnson (eds), *African Perspectives* (Cambridge 1970).
Bauer, P.T., *West African Trade* (Cambridge 1954).
Crowder, M., *West Africa Under Colonial Rule* (London 1968).
Crowder, M., *Colonial West Africa: Collected Essays* (London 1978).
Duignan, P. and L.H. Gann (eds), *Colonialism in Africa, 1870–1960* (5 vols Cambridge 1969–76).
Fage, J., *A History of Africa* (London 1978).
Frankel, S.H., *Capital Investment in Africa* (London 1938).
Gann, L.H. and P. Duignan, *Burden of Empire. An Appraisal of Western Colonialism South of the Sahara* (London 1968).
Gann, L.H. and P. Duignan (eds), *African Proconsuls: European Governors in Africa* (New York 1978).
Gann, L.H. and P. Duignan (eds), *The Rulers of British Africa, 1870–1914* (London 1979).
Gifford, P. and W.R. Louis (eds), *Britain and Germany in Africa* (New Haven Conn. 1967).
Gifford, P. and W.R. Louis (eds), *France and Britain in Africa* (New Haven Conn. 1971).
Hailey, Lord, *An African Survey* (London 1957).

Herskovitz, M.J. and M. Harwitz (eds), *Economic Transition in Africa* (London 1964).

Hetherington, P., *British Paternalism and Africa 1920-1940* (London 1978).

Hopkins, A.G., *An Economic History of West Africa* (London 1973).

Hunter, G., *Modernizing peasant societies: a comparative study in Asia and Africa* (Oxford 1969).

Jackson, E.F., *Economic Development in Africa* (Oxford 1965).

Jucker-Fleetwood, E.E., *Money and Finance in Africa* (London 1964).

Konczacki, Z.A. and J.M. Konczacki (eds), *An Economic History of Tropical Africa: the Colonial Period* (London 1977).

Lipschutz, M.R. and R.K. Rassmussen, *A Dictionary of African Historical Biography* (London 1978).

Lugard, Lord, *The Dual Mandate in British Tropical Africa* (London 1922).

Mair, L.P., *Native Policies in Africa* (London 1936).

Middleton, J., *The Effects of Economic Development on Traditional political Systems in Africa South Of The Sahara* (The Hague 1966).

Munro, J.F., *Africa and the International Economy, 1800-1960. An Introduction to the Modern Economic History of Africa South of the Sahara* (London 1976).

Neumark, S.D., *Foreign Trade and Economic Development in Africa: a Historical Perspective* (Stanford Calif. 1934).

Newbury, C.W., *British Policy Towards West Africa. Select Documents 1875-1914* (Oxford 1965).

Newbury, C.W., *The Western Slave Coast and its Rulers* (Oxford 1971).

Newlyn, W.T. and D.C. Rowan, *Money and Banking in British Colonial Africa* (Oxford 1954).

Nwabueze, B.O., *Judicialism in Commonwealth Africa. The Role of the Courts in Government* (London 1977).

Oliver, R. and A. Atmore, *Africa since 1800* (Cambridge 1967).

Poquin, J.-J., *Les Relations économiques extérieurs des pays d'Afrique Noire de l'union française* (Paris 1957).

Suret-Canale, J., *French Colonialism in Tropical Africa* (New York 1971).

Wilson, H.S., *The Imperial Experience in sub Saharan Africa Since 1870* (London 1977).

2. British Africa

a. British West Africa

Adeleye, R.A., *Power and Diplomacy in Northern Nigeria 1800-1906* (London 1969).

Apter, D.E., *The Gold Coast in Transition* (Princeton 1955).

Birmingham, W., I. Neustadt and E.N. Omaboe, (eds), *A Study of Contemporary Ghana* (London 1966).

Bourret, F.M., *Ghana: The Road to Independence, 1919–1957* (Stanford Calif. 1960).

Burns, A.C., *History of Nigeria* (London 1955).

Coleman, J.S., *Nigeria: Background to Nationalism* (Berkeley Calif. 1958).

Cox-George, N.A., *Finance and Development in West Africa* (London 1961).

Fage, J.D., *Ghana: a Historical Interpretation* (Madison 1959).

Flint, J.E., *Sir George Goldie and the Making of Nigeria* (London 1960).

Fyfe, C., *A History of Sierra Leone* (London 1962).

Genoud, R., *Nationalism and Economic Development in Ghana* (London 1969).

Heussler, R., *The British in Northern Nigeria* (London 1968).

Hill, P., *The Gold Coast Cocoa Farmers* (Cambridge 1956).

Ikime, O., *Niger Delta rivalry. Itsekiri-Urhobo relations and the European presence 1884–1938* (New York 1969).

Kilby, P., *Industrialization in an Open Economy: Nigeria 1945–1966* (Cambridge 1969).

Kimble, D., *A Political History of Ghana* (Oxford 1963).

Le Vine, V.T., *The Cameroons: from Mandate to Independence* (Berkeley Calif. 1964).

Nicolson, I.F., *The Administration of Nigeria 1900–1960: Men, Methods and Myths* (Oxford 1969).

Obichere, B.I., *Studies in Southern Nigerian History* (London 1978).

Perham, M. (ed.), *The Native Economics of Nigeria* (London 1946).

Perham, M. (ed.), *Mining, Commerce and Finance in Nigeria* (London 1948).

Perham, M. (ed.), *Lugard: The Years of Adventure 1858–1898* (London 1956).

Perham, M. (ed.), *Lugard: The Years of Authority 1898–1945* (London 1960).

Sokolski, A., *The Establishment of Manufacturing in Nigeria* (London 1965).

Szereszewski, R., *Structural Change in the Economy of Ghana, 1891–1911* (London 1965).

Wells, F.A., and W.A. Warmington, *Studies in Industrialization* (London 1962).

b. British South and Central Africa

Berger, E.L., *Labour, Race and Colonial Rule: The Copperbelt from 1925 to Independence* (Oxford 1974).

Cambridge History of the British Empire vol. VIII, *South Africa, Rhodesia and the High Commission Territories* (Cambridge 1963).

De Kiewiet, C.W., *A History of South Africa: Social and Economic* (Oxford 1941).

Gann, L.H., *A History of Northern Rhodesia* (London 1964).

Gann, L.H., *A History of Southern Rhodesia: Early Days to 1934* (London 1965).

Gray, R., *The Two Nations: Aspects of the Development of Race Relations in the Rhodesias and Nyasaland* (London 1960).

Jones, G.B., *Britain and Nyasaland* (London 1964).

Leys, C.T., *European Politics in Southern Rhodesia* (Oxford 1959).

Mason, P., *The Birth of a Dilemma: The Conquest and Settlement of Rhodesia* (London 1958).

McCracken, J., *Politics and Christianity in Malawi 1875–1940: The Impact of the Livingstonia mission in the Northern Province* (Cambridge 1977).

Roberts, A., *A History of Zambia* (London 1977).

Thompson, C.H. and H.W. Woodruff, *Economic Development in Rhodesia and Nyasaland* (London 1954).

Thompson, L.M., *The Unification of South Africa* (Oxfford 1960).

Walshe, P., *The Rise of African Nationalism in South Africa* (Berkeley 1971).

Wilson, M. and L. Thompson (eds), *The Oxford History of South Africa* (2 vols, Oxford 1969–71).

Windrich, E. (ed.), *Britain and the Politics of Rhodesian Independence* (London 1978).

c. British East Africa

Abd Al-Rahim, M., *Imperialism and Nationalism in the Sudan: A Study in Constitutional and Political Development 1899–1956* (Oxford 1969).

Austen, R.A., *Northwest Tanzania under German and British Rule 1889–1939* (New Haven 1968).

Bennett, G., *Kenya: a Political History* (London 1963).

Chidzero, B.T.G., *Tanganyika and International Trusteeship* (London 1961).

Coupland, R., *The Exploitation of East Africa 1856–1890* (Oxford 1939).

Dilley, M., *British Policy in Kenya Colony* (London 1966).

History of East Africa (3 vols, Oxford 1963–76).

Ingham, K., *The Making of Modern Uganda* (London 1958).

Ingham, K., *A History of East Africa* (London 1962).

Low, D.A., *Buganda in Modern History* (London 1971).

Morgan, D.J., *British Private Investment in East Africa* (London 1965).

Morgan, W.T.W., *East Africa, its People and Resources* (London 1971).

Morris, H.S., *The Indians in Uganda: Caste and Sect in a Plural Society* (London 1968).

Mungeam, G.H., *British Rule in Kenya, 1895–1912* (Oxford 1966).

Pearson, D.S., *Industrial Development in East Africa* (London 1969).

Stephens, H.W., *The Political Transformation of Tanganyika: 1920–67* (New York 1968).

Zwanenberg, R.M.A., *An Economic History of Kenya and Uganda, 1800–1970* (London 1975).

3. French Africa

a. French West and Equatorial Africa and Madagascar

Amin, S., *Le développement du Capitalisme en Côte d'Ivoire* (Paris 1967).

Amin, S., *L'Afrique de l'Ouest bloquée: l'Economic Politique de la Colonisation, 1880–1970* (Paris 1971).

Amin, S. and C. Coquery-Vidrovitch, *Histoire économique du Congo, 1880–1968* (Paris 1969).

Capet, M., *Traité d'Economie tropicale* (Paris 1958).

Cornevin, R., *Histoire du Togo* (Paris 1969).

Crowder, M., *Senegal: A Study of French Assimilation Policy* (London 1967).

Deschamps, H., *Histoire de Madagascar* (Paris 1960).

Hargreaves, J.D., *West Africa: The Former French States* (Englewood Cliffs N.J. 1967).

Hargreaves, J.D. (ed.), *France and West Africa* (London 1969).

Joseph, R.A., *Radical Nationalism in Cameroon: Social Origins of the UPC Rebellion* (London 1977).

Le Vine, V.T., *The Cameroons, from Mandate to Independence* (Berkeley Calif. 1964).

Morgenthau, R.S., *Political parties in French-speaking West Africa* (New York 1964).

Peterec, R.J., *Dakar and West African Economic Development* (New York 1967).

Rodney, W., *A History of the Upper Guinea Coast, 1545–1800* (London 1970).

Thompson, C.H. and H.W. Woodruff, *The Emerging States of French Equatorial Africa* (Stanford, Calif. 1960).

Thompson, V. and R. Adloff, *French West Africa* (London 1958).

Wagret, J.-M., *Histoire et sociologie politiques de la Republique du Congo (Brazzaville)* (Paris 1963).

b. French North Africa

Ayache, A., *Le Maroc* (Paris 1956).

Duwaji, G., *Economic Development in Tunisia* (London 1968).

Esquer, G., *Histoire de l'Algérie 1930–57* (Paris 1957).

Lacoste, Y., A. Nouschi, and A. Prenant, *L'Algérie passé et présent* (Paris 1961).

Stewart, C.F., *The Economy of Morocco 1912–1962* (Cambridge Mass. 1964).

Thompson, V. and R. Adloff, *Djibouti and the Horn of Africa* (Stanford Calif. 1968).

Tourneau, R. Le., *Evolution de l'Afrique du Nord musulmane 1920–61* (Paris 1961).

4. German Africa to 1919

Brunschwig, H., *L'Expansion Allemande outre-mer* (Paris 1957).

Gann, L.H. and P. Duignan, *The Rulers of German Africa, 1884–1914* (Stanford Calif. 1977).

Henderson, W.O., *Studies in German Colonial History* (London 1962).

Iliffe, J., *Tanganyika under German Rule, 1905–1912* (Cambridge 1969).

Louis, W.R., *Ruanda-Urundi, 1884–1919* (Oxford 1963).

Rudin, H.R., *Germans in the Cameroons, 1884–1914* (London 1938).

Stoecker, H. (ed.), *Kamerum unter deutscher Kolonialherrschaft* (Berlin 1960).

Townsend, M.E., *The Rise and Fall of Germany's Colonial Empire* (New York 1930).

5. Belgian Africa

Anstey, R., *King Leopold's Legacy: The Congo under Belgian Rule, 1908–1960* (London 1966).

Brausch, G., *Belgian Administration in the Congo* (London 1961).

Cornevin, R., *Histoire du Congo (Léopoldville-Kinshasa)* (Paris 1966).

Emerson, B., *Leopold II of the Belgians, King of Colonialism* (London 1979).

Franck, L., *Le Congo belge* (Brussels 1928).

Gann, L.H. and Duignan, P., *The Rulers of Belgian Africa, 1884–1914* (Princeton N.J. 1979).

Lacroix, J.-L., *Industrialisation au Congo* (Paris 1966).

Lemarchand, R., *Political awakening in the Belgian Congo* (London 1964).

Ryckmans, P., *La politique coloniale* (Louvain 1934).

Slade, R., *King Leopold's Congo* (London 1962).

Stengers, J., *Combien le Congo u-t-il coûte a la Belgique?* (Brussels 1957).

Van der Kerken, G., *La Politique coloniale Belge* (Antwerp 1943).

Vandewalle, G., *De Conjuncturele Evolutie in Kongo en Ruanda-Urundi van 1920 tot 1939 en van 1949 tot 1958* (Antwerp 1966).

6. Portuguese Africa

Abshire, D.M. and M.A. Samuels (eds), *Portuguese Africa: A Handbook* (London 1969).

Bender, G.J., *Angola Under the Portuguese: the Myth and the Reality* (London 1978).

Casimiro, A., *Angola e o Fututo* (Lisbon 1958).

Chilcote, R.H., *Emerging Nationalism in Portuguese Africa: Documents* (Stanford Calif. 1972).

Duffy, J., *Portuguese Africa* (Cambridge Mass. 1959).

Figueiredo, A. De, *Portugal and its Empire: the Truth* (London 1961).

Hammond, R.J., *Portugal and Africa, 1815–1910* (Stanford Calif. 1966).

Wheeler, D.J. and R. Pélissier, *Angola* (New York 1971).

7. Italian Africa

Baer, G.W., *The Coming of the Italo-Ethiopian War* (Cambridge Mass. 1967).

Becker, G.H., *The Disposition of the Italian Colonies, 1941–1951* (Annemasse 1952).

Dainelli, G., *Gli Esploratori Italiani in Africa* (Turin 1960).

Del Boca, A., *La Guerra d'Abissinia (1935–41)* (Milan 1965).

Hess, R.L., *Italian Colonialism in Somalia* (Chicago 1966).

Howard, W.E.H., *Public Administration in Ethiopia: A Study in Retrospect and Prospect* (Groningen 1956).

Leone, E. de, *La Colonizzazione deli'Africa del Nord* (Padua 1960).

Longrigg, S.H., *A Short History of Eritrea* (Oxford 1945).

Miège, J.L., *L'impérialisme colonial italien de 1870 à nos jours* (Paris 1968).

Rainero, R., *I primi teutatari di colonizzazione agricola e di Popolamento deli'Eritrea, 1880–90* (Milan 1960).

Segre, C., *Fourth shore. The Italian Colonization of Libya* (Chicago 1974).

Varley, D.H., *A Bibliography of Italian Colonization in Africa* (London 1970).

Zoli, C., *Espansione coloniale italiana* (Rome 1949).

III. Colonialism in the Middle East

Abdel-Malek, A., *Idéologie et Renaissance nationale: l'Egypt moderne* (Paris 1969).

Ahmed, J.M., *The Intellectual Origins of Egyptian Nationalism* (London 1960).

Bullard, Sir R., *Britain and the Middle East: From the Earliest Times to 1950* (London 1951).

Colombe, M., *L'evolution de l'egypte: 1923–50* (Paris 1951).

Farnie, D.A., *East and West of Suez: The Suez Canal in History 1854–1956* (London 1969).

Hourani, A., *Arabic Thought in the Liberal Age 1789–1939* (London 1962).

Issawi, C.P. and M. Yeganeh, *The Economics of Middle Eastern Oil* (London 1963).

Keddie, N.R., *Religion and Rebellion in Iran* (London 1966).

Landes, D.S., *Bankers and Pashas* (London 1958).

Lenczowski, G., *Oil and State in the Middle East* (Ithaca 1960).

Longrigg, S., *Iraq, 1900–1950* (London 1953).

Longrigg, S., *Syria and Lebanon Under French Mandate* (London 1958).

Longrigg, S., *Oil in the Middle East: Its Discovery and Development* (London 1961).

Marlowe, J., *Anglo-Egyptian Relations, 1800–1953* (London 1954).

Marlowe, J., *Arab Nationalism and British Imperialism* (London 1961).

Mikdashi, Z., *A Financial Analysis of Middle Eastern Oil Concessions: 1901–1965* (London 1966).

Monroe, E., *Britain's Moment in the Middle East, 1914–56* (London 1963).

Owen, E.R.J., *Cotton and the Egyptian Economy, 1820–1914* (Oxford 1969).

Vatikiotis, P.J., *The Modern History of Egypt* (London 1980).

Williams, E., *Britain and France in the Middle East and North Africa 1914–1967* (London 1968).

IV. Colonialism in Asia

1. India and Ceylon (Sri Lanka)

Anstey, V., *The Economic Development of India* (4th ed. London 1952).

Appadorai, A. (ed.), *Documents on Political Thought in Modern India* (London 1973).

Bagchi, A.K., *Private Investment in India, 1900–1939* (Cambridge 1972).

Bailey, S.D., *Ceylon* (London 1952).

Ballhatchet, *Race, Sex and Class under the Raj* (London 1980).

Blyn, G., *Agricultural Trends in India, 1891–1947* (Philadelphia 1966).

Brecher, M., *Nehru: A Political Biography* (London 1959).

Buchanan, D.H., *The Development of Capitalist Enterprise in India* (London 1966).

Cambridge History of India vol. VI, *The Indian Empire, 1858–1918* (Cambridge 1932).

Chamberlain, M.E., *Britain and India: the Interaction of Two Peoples* (Newton Abbot 1974).

Dilks, D., *Curzon in India* (2 vols, London 1969–70).

Griffiths, Sir P., *The British Impact on India* (London 1952).

Gunasekera, H.A. de S., *From Dependent Currency to Central Banking in Ceylon* (London 1962).

Hirsch, L.V., *Marketing in an Underdeveloped Economy: the North Indian Sugar Industry* (Englewood Cliffs N.J. 1961).

Islam, N., *Foreign Capital and Economic Development, Japan, India and Canada* (Rutland Vermont 1960).

Johnson, G., *Provincial Politics and Indian Nationalism: Bombay and the Indian National Congress, 1880–1915* (Cambridge 1973).

Kidron, M., *Foreign Investments in India* (London 1965.

Kumar, R., *Western India and the Nineteenth Century* (London 1968).

Low, D.A. (ed.), *Congress and the Raj* (London 1978).

Masselos, J., *Nationalism on the Indian Sub-continent: An Introductory History* (Melbourne 1972).

Mendis, G.C., *Ceylon under the British* (Colombo 1944).

Mills, L.A., *Ceylon under British Rule* (London 1933).

Misra, B.B., *The Indian Middle Classes* (London 1961).

Moore, R.J., *Liberalism and Indian Politics, 1872–1922* (London 1966).

Morris, M.D., *The Emergence of an Industrial Labour Force in India* (Berkeley and Los Angeles 1965).

Nanda, B.R., *Gokhale: the Indian Moderates and the British Raj* (London 1977).

Neale, W.C., *Economic Change in Rural India* (New Haven 1962).

Panikkar, K., *A Survey of Indian History* (Bombay 1947).

Philips, C.H. (ed.), *The Evolution of India and Pakistan, 1858–1947* (London 1962).

Philips, C.H. and M.W. Wainwright (eds), *Indian Society and the Beginnings of Modernization* (London 1976).

Raj, J., *The Mutiny and British Land Policy in North India, 1856–68* (London 1965).

Ray, R.K., *Industrialization in India. Growth and Conflict in the Private Corporate Sector 1914–47* (Delhi 1979).

Robb, P.G., *The Government of India and Reform: Policies Towards Politics and the Constitution, 1916–1921* (London 1977).

Seal, A., *The Emergence of Indian Nationalism* (Cambridge 1968).

Silver, A., *Manchester Men and Indian Cotton, 1847–72* (Manchester 1966).

Singh, V.B. (ed.), *Economic History of India, 1857–1956* (Bombay 1965).

Sinha, N.K., *Economic History of Bengal* (Calcutta 1956).

Spear, T.G.P., *India: A Modern History* (Ann Arbor Mich. 1962).

Symonds, R., *The Making of Pakistan* (London 1951).

Thorner, D., *Investment in Empire* (Philadelphia 1950).

Thorner, D. and A. Thorner, *Land and Labour in India* (Bombay 1962).

Tomlinson, B.R., *The Political Economy of the Raj, 1914–1947* (London 1979).

2. South-East Asia

Allen, G.C. and A.G. Donnithorne, *Western Enterprise in Indonesia and Malaya* (London 1957).

Allen, Sir R., *Malaysia, Prospect and Retrospect: The Impact and Aftermath of Colonial Rule* (London 1968).

Arx, A. van, *L'évolution politique en Indonésie de 1900 à 1942* (Paris 1949).

Bauer, P.T., *The Rubber Industry* (London 1948).

Boeke, J.H., *The Structure of Netherlands Indian Economy* (New York 1942).

Boeke, J.H., *The Evolution of the Netherlands Indian Economy* (New York 1946).

Buttinger, J., *The Smaller Dragon: A Political History of Vietnam* (New York 1958).

Cady, J.F., *A History of Modern Burma* (Ithaca 1958).

Chai Hon Chan, *The Development of British Malaya, 1896–1909* (Kuala Lumpur 1964).

Cheng Siok, Hwa, *The Rice Industry of Burma 1852–1940* (1968).

Cowan, C.D. (ed.), *The Economic Development of South-East Asia* (London 1964).

Dahm, B., *History of Indonesia in the Twentieth Century* (London 1971).

Devillers, P., *Histoire du Vietnam de 1940 à 1952* (Paris 1952).

Drabble, J., *Rubber in Malaya, 1876–1922* (Kuala Lumpur 1973).

Duncanson, D.J., *Government and Revolution in Vietnam* (London 1968).

Emerson, R., *Malaysia. A Study in Direct and Indirect Rule* (New York 1937).

Furnivall, J.S., *Netherlands India* (Cambridge 1944).

Furnivall, J.S., *Colonial Policy and Practice: A Comparative Study of Burma and Netherlands India* (Cambridge 1948).

Furnivall, J.S., *The Governance of Burma* (New York 1960).

Galembert, J. de, *Les Administrations et les Services Publics indochinois* (Hanoi 1931).

Gethyn Davies, S., *Central Banking in South and East Asia* (Hong Kong 1960).

Hall, D.G.E., *Burma* (London 1950).

Hall, D.G.E., *A History of South-East Asia* (London 1955).

Hoang-van-Chi, *From Colonialism to Communism; A Case Study of North Vietnam* (London 1964).

Ho-Chi-Minh, *Le procès de la Colonisation française* (Paris 1926).

Jackson, J., *Planters and Speculators. Chinese and European Agricultural Enterprise in Malaya, 1786–1921* (Singapore 1963).

Kahin, G.M., *Nationalism and Revolution in Indonesia* (Ithaca 1952).

Kat Angelino, A.D.A. de, *Colonial Policy* (The Hague 1931).

Le Thanh Khoi, *Le Viet-nam, Histoire et Civilisation* (Paris 1955).

Masson, A., *Histoire de l'Indochine* (Paris 1950).

Palmier, L.H., *Indonesia and the Dutch* (London 1962).
Purcell, V., *The Chinese in Malaya* (London 1960).
Robequain, C., *The Economic Development of French Indo-China* (Oxford 1944).
Roff, W.R., *The Origins of Malay Nationalism* (New Haven Conn. 1967).
Sadka, E., *The Protected Malay States, 1874–1895* (Kuala Lumpur 1968).
Sandhu, K.S., *Indians in Malaya, 1786–1957* (Cambridge 1969).
Tarling, N., *Britain, the Brookes and Borneo* (Kuala Lumpur 1971).
Tinker, H., *South Asia* (London 1966).
Vlekke, B.H.M., *Nusantara. A History of the East Indian Archipelago* (Cambridge Mass. 1944).

V. Colonialism in the Pacific

Belshaw, C.S., *Island Administration in the South West Pacific* (London 1950).
Bourgeau, J., *La France du Pacifique* (Paris 1950).
Coulter, J.W., *The Pacific Dependencies of the United States* (New York 1957).
Day, A. G., *Hawaii and its People* (New York 1955).
Day, A.G. and R.S. Kuykendall, *Hawaii, a History from Polynesian Kingdom to American Commonwealth* (New York 1948).
Dodge, E.S., *Islands and Empires: Western Impact on the Pacific and East Asia* (London 1978).
Forbes, W.C., *The Philippine Islands* (Cambridge Mass. 1945).
Gillion, K.L., *Fiji's Indian Migrants: A History to the End of Indenture in 1920* (Melbourne 1962).
Gilson, R.P., *Samoa, 1830–1930: The Politics of a Multiracial Community* (Melbourne 1970).
Gratton, C.H., *The South West Pacific* (Ann Arbor Mich. 1963).
Legge, J.D., *Australian Colonial Policy* (Sydney 1956).
Legge, J.D., *Britain in Fiji, 1858–1880* (London 1958).
Morrell, W.P., *Britain in the Pacific Islands* (Oxford 1960).
Parnaby, D.W., *Britain and the Labour Trade in the South West Pacific* (Durham N.C. 1964).
Scarr, D., *Fragments of Empire. A History of the Western Pacific High Commission, 1877–1914* (Canberra 1968).
Thompson, L., *Guam and its People* (Princeton N.J. 1947).

VI. The Caribbean colonies

Beachey, R.W., *The British West Indies Sugar Industry in the Late 19th Century* (Oxford 1957).

Blanshard, P., *Democracy and Empire in the Caribbean* (New York 1947).

Knight, F.W., *The Caribbean: The Genesis of a Fragmented Nationalism* (New York 1978).

Lewis, G.K., *The Growth of the Modern West Indies* (London 1968).

Mitchell, Sir H., *Europe in the Caribbean* (Edinburgh 1963).

O'Loughlin, C., *Economic and Political Change in the Leeward and Windward Islands* (New Haven Conn. 1968).

Parry, J.H. and P.M. Sherlock, *A Short History of the West Indies* (London 1956).

Perkins, D., *The United States and the Caribbean* (London 1947).

Revert, E., *La France d'Amérique* (Paris 1949).

Tugwell, R.G., *The Stricken Land: the Story of Puerto Rico* (Garden City New Jersey 1947).

Waddell, D.A.G., *The West Indies and Guiana* (Englewood Cliffs N.J. 1967).

Will, H.A., *Constitutional Change in the British West Indies, 1880–1903* (Oxford 1971).

IV. A Short Chronology of Colonialism 1870-1945

Date	Place	Event
1871		
March	Algeria	Revolt of Sidi Mokrani.
October	South Africa	Britain annexed the diamond-producing area at Kimberley.
1872		
February	Gold Coast	The Netherlands sold its trading forts to Britain.
1873		
April– February 1874	Gold Coast	British expedition against Ashanti, which ended with a treaty by which Ashanti promised freedom for trade.
June	Zanzibar	The Sultan abolished slave markets and the export of slaves under pressure from the British Consul, Sir John Kirk.
21 December	Tonkin	Francis Garnier killed by Chinese troops during expedition to Hanoi.
1874		
15 March	Annam	Franco-Annamese treaty giving France a protectorate over Annam and commercial access to southern China.
25 October	Fiji	Britain annexed Fiji group at invitation of the paramount chief, Thakombau.
1875		
25 November	Egypt	Britain bought 7/16ths of Suez Canal Company shares from the Khedive.
1876		
8 April	Egypt	The Khedive suspended payment on treasury bills, leading to establishment of the international Caisse de la Dette publique which resulted in the Anglo-French Dual Control of 1879.

September	Congo	Brussels Conference led to foundation of Association Internationale Africaine by Leopold II of the Belgians

1877

12 March	South-West Africa	Britain annexed Walvis Bay.
9 April	Congo	H.M. Stanley reached coast after exploration of the Congo river.
12 April	Transvaal	Britain annexed the Transvaal to Cape Colony.

1878

June–July	Berlin	Berlin Congress on the future of the Ottoman empire, leading the Treaty of Berlin. Turkey agreed to British possession of Cyprus.
25 November	Congo	Comité d'Etudes du HautCongo formed by Leopold II to finance occupation of Congo.

1879

January–July	South Africa	Anglo-Zulu war led to end of Zulu power.
24 January	Samoa	German–Samoan treaty marked start of international rivalry in South Pacific.

1880

29 June	Tahiti	France annexed Tahiti, previously a protectorate.
June	Congo	S. de Brazza established French post at Franceville to counter Stanley's treaty-making on behalf of Leopold II.

1881

12 May	Tunis	The Bey of Tunis signed the protectorate treaty of Bardo with France after French invasion from Algeria.
August	South Africa	By the Pretoria convention Britain recognized the independence of the Transvaal.
September	Egypt	Nationalist movement under Col. Arabi against actions of the Dual Control.
September	Annam	Start of war between France and China over Tonkin
December	Congo	Stanley founded Leopoldville.

1882

25 April	Annam	Hanoi occupied by French troops.
June–September	Egypt	British bombardment of Alexandria after riots, defeat of Egyptian army at Tel-el-Kebir and start of British occupation, ending Dual Control with France.
December	Eritrea	Italian occupation of Assab began Italian colonization in Africa.

1883

June–December 1885	Madagascar	French invasion, ending with protectorate.
August	Annam	Treaty of Hué gave France effective control (revised June 1884, leading to Federation of Indo-China in 1887).
November	Egyptian Sudan	The Mahdi defeated Egyptian troops at El Obeid. Britain decided to evacuate the Sudan.

1884

April	South-West Africa	German protectorate declared.
14 July	Siam	Anglo-French treaty on the Mekong basin.
November–February 1885	Berlin	Berlin Conference on the partition of Africa.

1885

26 January	Sudan	Death of General Charles Gordon at Khartoum.
5 February	Congo	Establishment of the Congo Free State.
6 February	Eritrea	Italy occupied Massawa.
25 February	Tanganyika	German protectorate declared over Tanganyika.
17 March	New Guinea	Germany declared protectorate over Northern New Guinea and adjacent islands.
31 March	Bechuanaland	Britain declared protectorate over Northern Bechuanaland.
5 June	Nigeria	Britain declared protectorate over Lower Niger river area.

28 November	Burma	British occupied Mandalay, leading to annexation of kingdom of Upper Burma, January, 1886.
December	India	Indian National Congress founded.

1886

29 June	Gabon	Establishment of French colonies of Gabon and Congo.
10 July	Nigeria	Charter given to Royal Niger Company.
July–November	Africa	Anglo-German agreements delimiting their interests in West and East Africa.

1887

16 November	New Hebrides	Anglo-French condominium over New Hebrides agreed.

1888

12 May	North Borneo	British protectorate declared.

1889

10 January	Ivory Coast	French protectorate declared.
2 May	Ethiopia	Italian treaty signed with Ras Menelik.
June–July	Brussels	Conference on slavery, etc. leading to Brussels Act.
5 August	West Africa	Anglo-French agreement on boundaries.
October	South Africa	Charter granted to Rhodes' British South Africa Company.

1890

1 July	East Africa	Anglo-German agreement over East Africa. Heligoland ceded to Germany.

1891

24 March	Ethiopia	Anglo-Italian agreement over Ethiopia.

1892

3 December	West Africa	French protectorate over Dahomey, leading to this, Guinea and the Ivory Coast becoming French possessions in March 1893.

1893

3 October	Siam	Siam ceded left bank of River Mekong to France.
15 November	West Africa	Anglo-German agreement defining frontiers.

1894

5 May	East Africa	Anglo-Italian agreement on boundaries.
17 July	Ethiopia	Start of Italian expedition to occupy Ethiopia.
November	Madagascar	French expedition began conquest, leading to annexation of the island in August 1886.

1895

29 December	Transvaal	Jameson raid on Johannesburg failed.

1896

1 March	Ethiopia	Defeat of Italian forces at Adowa, leading to fall of Crispi government on 5 March.
June	Sudan	Start of the Marchand mission from Gabon to the Nile at Fashoda.
August	Philippines	Start of rising against Spanish rule.

1897

November	China	Germany occupied Kiao-Chow Bay as naval base.

1898

24 April	Cuba	USA declared war on Spain after sinking of US naval vessel at Havana, leading to conquest of Cuba, Puerto Rico, the Philippines, etc.
10 July	Sudan	Marchand reached Fashoda and raised tricolour.
September	Sudan	Kitchener destroyed Mahdist army at Omdurman and confronted Marchand at Fashoda.
4 November	Sudan	France decided to evacuate Fashoda to avoid danger of war with Britain.
10 December	USA and Spain	Treaty of Paris. Spain ceded Cuba, Puerto Rico, the Philippines and Guam.

1899

21 March	Sudan	Anglo-French agreement over the Egyptian Sudan.
12 October	South Africa	Start of Anglo-Boer War, ending in May 1902 with the Peace of Vereeniging by which Britain annexed the Transvaal and Orange Free State.

1900

| 14 December | Morocco | Secret Franco-Italian agreement giving France first claim to Morocco and Italy to Tripolitania. |

1903

| May | Congo | Start of campaign by E.D. Morel and R. Casement to publicize defects of rule in Congo Free State. |

1904

4 February	Far East	Outbreak of Russo-Japanese War, resulting in defeat of Russia in 1905 and Japanese occupation of Manchuria.
October	West Africa	Creation of Federation of French West Africa (AOF).
8 April	France, Britain	Signing of Anglo-French Entente which resolved all outstanding disputes over colonial issues.

1905

| 31 March | Morocco | First Moroccan crisis: William II arrived at Tangiers as protest against French influence in Morocco. |
| | India | Partition of Bengal by Lord Curzon agitates Indian nationalists. Bengal reunited in 1911. |

1906

16 January–7 April	Morocco	Algeciras Conference on future of Morocco, leading to Algeciras Act guaranteeing its independence but giving France and Spain special rights there.
4 July	Ethiopia	Anglo-French-Italian agreement on independence of Ethiopia.
6 December	South Africa	Transvaal and Orange Free State given self-government, leading to creation of Union of South Africa as Dominion in 1910.

1907

| September | South-West Africa | Start of Herero rising against German rule, resulting in massacre of Hereros. |

1908

| 25 June | French Equatorial Africa | Gabon, Congo and other territories federated as French Equatorial Africa (AEF). |

20 August	Congo	Congo Free State transferred to Belgium as a colony following criticism of rule by Leopold II.

1909

	India	Introduction of Morley-Minto Reforms, giving increased Indian participation in central and provincial government.

1911

4 May	Morocco	French troops occupied the capital, Fez, at request of Sultan, leading to German gunboat *Panther* arriving at Agadir on 1 July in protest.
4 November	Morocco	Franco-German agreement that Morocco be divided between France and Spain, subject to rights of other nations, and Germany should receive part of AEF in compensation.
5 November	Morocco	Italy occupied Tripolitania, leading to Treaty of Lausanne, 18 October 1912, by which Turkey recognized Italian ownership.

1914

1 January	Nigeria	North and South Nigeria united under a single governor-General.
1–4 August	Europe	Outbreak of First World War.
8 August	Togo	British and French troops occupied Togo.
15 September	New Guinea	Germans capitulated to Australians.
5 November	Cyprus	Britain annexed Cyprus as Turkey an enemy.
17 December	Egypt	British protectorate declared.

1915

21 May	Europe	Italy declared war on Austria-Hungary.
9 July	South-West Africa	German authorities capitulated to South Africans.

1916

18 February	Cameroons	Germans capitulated to British and French.
4 September	Tanganyika	Dar-es-Salam taken by British troops.

1917

| | India | Britain announced aim of self-government for India, resulting in Montagu-Chelmsford Reforms of 1918. |

2 November   Palestine   Balfour Declaration promised a national home for the Jews in Palestine.

1918

11 November   Europe   Armistice ended First World War.

1919

18 January–   Europe   Versailles·Peace Conference, leading to
28 June   signature of the Treaty of Versailles. Germany lost all overseas possessions which were to be distributed among the allies as mandates of the League of Nations.

1920

8 July   Kenya   British East Africa divided into colony of Kenya and protectorate of Uganda.

August   India   Gandhi began non-cooperation movement to achieve home rule.

1921

3 January   India   First meeting of new all-Indian parliament; India given fiscal and tariff autonomy.

13 December   Pacific   Washington Agreement between USA, Britain, Japan and France on territories in the Pacific.

1922

21 February   Egypt   Anglo-Egyptian treaty ended the protectorate.

20 July   League of Nations Council approved British and French mandates over Togo, Cameroons, Tanganyika and Palestine.

24 August   Palestine   Arab Congress rejected the British mandate over Palestine.

1923

31 August   Ruanda-   League of Nations gave Belgium the
Urundi   mandate for Ruanda-Urundi.

1925

18 July–   Syria   Rising against French rule under mandate.
June 1927

1926

| November–July 1927 | Java | Communist rising against Dutch rule. |

1928

| 2 August | Ethiopia | Treaty of friendship between Italy and Ethiopia. |

1930

March	India	Gandhi started first civil disobedience campaign.
30 June	Iraq	Britain recognized independence of Iraq.
1 October	China	Britain evacuated the base at Wei-Hai-Wei.
12 November–January 1931	India	Round Table Conference on Indian self-government.

1931

| December | British Commonwealth | The Statute of Westminster defined the status of the Dominions (Canada, South Africa, New Zealand, Newfoundland and Eire) and allowed them to claim full sovereignty. |

1932

| July | Ottawa | Conference of Britain and the Dominions arranged system of imperial tariff preferences. |

1933

| 13 January | Philippines | US Congress voted that the Philippines should become independent in ten years (extended to 1946 due to the war). |

1934

| 5 December | Ethiopia | Incident on border between Ethiopia and Italian Somaliland led to constant friction. |

1935

2 August	India	Government of India Act (1) separated Burma and Aden from India; (2) created new constitution for India to start in 1937 with full self-government in the provinces.
2 October	Ethiopia	The Italians invaded Ethiopia.
19 October	Ethiopia	League of Nations decided to impose sanctions on Italy.

1936

5 May	Ethiopia	Italian forces occupied Addis Ababa.
15 July	Ethiopia	League of Nations ended sanctions against Italy.
26 August	Egypt	Anglo-Egyptian treaty redefined British rights in Egypt.
9 September	Syria	Franco-Syrian protocol promised Syria independence in 1939.

1937

20 November	Tunisia	Start of Neo-Dastur rising against French rule.

1939

3 September	Europe	Britain and France declared war on Germany.

1940

September	Indo-China	Japanese forces invaded Indo-China.

1941

January–September	Ethiopia and Somaliland	British forces occupied Italian East Africa.
June	Syria	Free French forces occupied Syria and ended mandate.
7 December	Pacific	Japanese attack on Pearl Harbor began war.
25 December	Hong Kong	Japanese forces occupied Hong Kong.

1942

	East	Japanese occupied British, French, American and Dutch possessions in South-east Asia and West Pacific.
April	India	Congress rejected offer of self-government after the war made by Cripps mission on ground that it was incomplete.

1944

January	Brazzaville	Conference held by Free French on future of French Africa.

1945

8 May	Europe	Germany capitulated.
2 September	The Pacific	Japan capitulated.

Index

Notes are indexed, but not the bibliography or chronological table. Authors referred to in Chapter III, *The Historiography of Modern Colonialism* are indexed only when they have been referred to earlier in the text.

Aden, 21
Africa, 2, 6, 11, 14, 17, 30, 35, 44, 46–7, 48, 62, 68, 70, 72, 74, 82, 88, 96, 99, 105, 106, 107, 110, 114, 115, 120
See also: Central Africa; East Africa; North Africa; North-east Africa; South-west Africa; southern Africa; West Africa
agriculture, 58, 68, 71, 77, 78–88, 92, 96, 97, 98
Algeria, 5, 13, 37, 39, 40
America, 4, 39, 40, 49, 51, 56, 59, 64, 65, 72, 94
See also: North America; United States
Angola, 4, 5, 40
Argentina, 9
Asia, 2, 5, 15, 61, 62, 82, 91, 103, 120
See also: South Asia; South-east Asia; southern Asia
assimilation, 36, 37–8, 113
association, principle, 38, 113
Australia, 5, 6, 18, 30, 72, 79

Belgium, 13, 16, 26, 39, 41, 53, 56, 59, 61, 65, 68, 73, 74, 76, 78, 79, 80, 89, 92, 95–100, 115, 116–17
Borneo, 33
Britain, British Empire, 5, 6, 8, 12, 16, 18, 21, 25, 26, 29–35, 36, 37, 38, 39, 40, 41, 53, 67, 75, 78, 84, 86, 89, 91, 92, 93, 94, 95, 99, 109, 111, 113–15, 116, 119
monetary policy, 61–65, 66
tariff policy, 53–60

British East Africa, *see* East Africa
British West Africa, *see* West Africa
Burma, 13, 33, 49, 72, 116

Cameroons, 18, 41
Cameroun, 85
Canada, 30, 64, 77, 101, 115
Caribbean, 36, 37, 66, 72, 79, 96, 110, 120
Central Africa, 5, 63, 91
Ceylon (Sri Lanka), 24, 28, 31, 33, 49, 72, 79, 103, 109
China, 8, 15, 21, 45, 46, 60, 72, 92, 106
Colonial Ministry, French, 26
Colonial Office, British, 26, 27, 35
Colonial Sterling Exchange Standard, 63, 64
colonies incorporées, 36
colonization, 1, 4–5, 11, 20, 40, 123
Congo, 67, 90
Belgian, 41, 53, 61, 65, 68, 74, 76, 78, 79, 80; industrialization in, 89, 92, 95–100, 116–17
French, 75, 102
conseils coloniaux, 37
conseils d'administration, 37
conseils de gouvernement, 37, 41
conseils généraux, 37
Crown Colony system, 30–1, 37
Cuba, 21
Cyprus, 21

Dahomey, 47
decolonization, 1, 2, 3, 5, 10, 11, 12, 13, 24, 29, 31, 35, 39, 49, 52, 64, 65, 97, 105, 109, 116, 118, 121

délégations, 37
direct rule, 31–3, 41
Dutch, *see* Netherlands

East Africa, 79, 80, 91, 100, 115
  British, 18, 63
  German, 18, 40
Egypt, 13, 33, 46, 47
Ethiopia, 13, 26, 47
Europe, 1, 2, 6, 7, 13, 15, 24, 44, 45,
  46, 48, 52, 68, 69–70, 71, 89, 103,
  104, 105, 112, 122
European Economic Community, 56
Exchange Equalization Account, 64

Fiji, 33
France, French Empire, 4, 5, 12, 16,
  17, 26, 28, 29, 36–9, 40, 41, 43, 44,
  50, 52, 53, 75, 84–8, 92, 100–2, 107,
  111, 112, 113, 114, 115–16, 119,
  122
  monetary policy, 61, 62, 65–6
  tariff policy, 56–7, 59
free trade, 28, 55–60, 89, 90
French Congo, *see* Congo
French Equatorial Africa, 56, 85
French Somali, 66
French North Africa, *see* North Africa
French West Africa, *see* West Africa

Gambia, 33
Germany, 18, 26, 39, 40, 41, 56, 104,
  117–18
Gold Coast (Ghana), 13, 14, 53, 55,
  75, 80, 82, 88, 102

Hawaii, 40
Hong Kong, 60, 72

imperialism, 1–4, 6, 11, 20, 21, 112,
  123
India, 6, 8, 15, 24, 28, 30, 32, 34, 49,
  53, 55, 57, 58–9, 61–2, 65, 70, 72,
  78, 79, 80, 81, 83–4, 103, 106, 107,
  109, 114
  industrialization in, 89, 90, 91, 92–5,
  98, 99, 100

India Office, 26, 115
Indian Ocean, 4, 72
indirect rule, 31–5, 38, 41, 113
Indo-China, 37, 49, 65, 66, 79
Indonesia, 4, 13, 24, 28, 41, 49, 61, 65,
  79, 80, 90, 95, 99, 103, 110
industrialization, 57, 59, 60, 68–9, 78,
  88–103, 104
  in Belgian Congo, 89, 95–100
  in French West Africa, 89, 92, 100–2
  in India, 89, 90, 91, 92–5, 98, 99, 100
Iraq, 18, 33
Italy, 5, 13, 17, 22, 26, 39, 40, 41, 59,
  65, 69, 106, 118
Ivory Coast, 57, 75, 79, 88, 101, 102

Japan, 18, 45, 46, 89
Java, 40, 70
Jordan, 18

Kenya, 5, 19, 30–1, 33, 75, 79, 99,
  102

labour policy, 69–74, 81, 103
land policy, 69, 74–6, 103
Latin America, 9, 10, 104
League of Nations, 12, 18, 19
Lenin, V. I, *Imperialism, the Highest
  Stage of Capitalism* (1916), 1, 6, 8,
  50, 112, 122
Leopold II of the Belgians, 13, 41, 116
Lever, William, 74
  Huileries du Congo Belge, 73, 76,
  99, 106
Libya, 5, 40, 41, 69
Lugard, Lord, 33, 117
  *The Dual Mandate in British
  Tropical Africa* (1922), 38, 50, 52,
  106, 113

Madagascar, 37
Malaya, 17, 33, 72, 79, 80
mandates, 18–19, 36
Mandates Commission, 18
Mauritius, 33
monetary policy, 54, 60–6
Morocco, 13, 17, 46, 56

Mozambique, 4, 5, 40, 72, 76
Mussolini, Benito, 22, 26, 40

neo-colonialism, 1, 2, 4, 8–10, 53
neo-mercantilist systems, 56, 89
Netherlands, 4, 13–14, 16, 26, 39, 40,
    41, 55, 59, 61, 65, 70, 85, 109–110,
    116
New Zealand, 5, 18, 30, 79
Nigeria, 8, 12, 33, 35, 47, 80, 88, 100,
    102
North Africa, 13, 61, 65, 120
    French, 66, 79
    Italian, 79
North America, 1, 2, 9, 46, 48, 68, 89,
    105, 122
North-east Africa, 5, 40, 65
Nyasaland (Malawi), 18, 33, 68

Oceania, 37

Pacific, 2, 6, 11, 17, 21, 30, 35, 37, 48,
    66, 71, 72, 79, 96, 120
Pakistan, 59
Palestine, 18, 63
Philippines, 4, 117
plantations, 21, 73, 74, 75, 76, 79, 80–
    1, 82
Portugal, 4, 16, 26, 39, 40, 56, 59, 65,
    72, 74, 76, 117
protected states, 17–18, 36
protectionism, 28, 56, 58, 60, 92
protectorates, 17–18, 20, 21, 36

Réunion, 36, 37, 40
Rhodesia, Southern (Zimbabwe), 5, 68,
    75, 96, 99
    Northern (Zambia), 33, 68, 75, 99
Ruanda-Urundi, 18

Sarraut, Albert, 28, 50, 113, 117
Schumpeter, J. A., 3, 20, 50
'self-government', 27, 29–31, 37
Senegal, 37

Sierra Leone, 33, 74
South Africa, 5, 18, 72, 75, 79, 96, 102
South Asia, 11, 35, 70
South Korea, 60
South-east Asia, 6, 11, 13, 30, 35, 45,
    70, 72, 73, 106
South-west Africa, 18, 40
southern Africa, 5, 33
southern Asia, 69, 71
Spain, 4, 16, 26, 39, 40, 56, 59
Sudan, 82, 83
Sumatra, 72
Suret-Canale, Jean, 9, 52, 85, 86, 106,
    107
Syria, 18

Tahiti, 36
Taiwan, 60
Tanganyika, 18, 19, 30, 33
tariffs, 54–60, 69, 90, 94, 100, 103
Tata, J. H., 94
taxation, 22, 34, 70, 74
Togoland, 18, 85
Tonga, 17, 33
trust territories, 18–19
trusteeship, 27
Trusteeship Council, 19
Tunis, 13, 17, 39, 46, 56
Turkey, 8, 15, 18, 45, 46

Uganda, 30, 33, 35
underdevelopment theory, 9–10, 45, 51,
    105
Unilever, 85, 99, 100, 106
United States, 6, 40, 46, 79, 140
United Nations, 12, 19

West Africa, 15, 21, 46–7, 70, 73, 80,
    82, 91, 99
    British, 18, 33, 52, 63, 75, 84, 86
    French, 52, 53, 56, 57, 75, 78, 79,
    84–8; industrialization in, 89, 92,
    100–2
West Indies, 28, 33, 63, 81